SCHOLASTIC

W9-AMB-809

SYSTEM 44

*NEXT*GENERATION

Decodable Digest

Credits appear on page 288, which constitutes an extension of this copyright page.

Copyright © 2009 by Scholastic Inc.
Previously published as *System 44 Decodable Digest*.

All rights reserved.   Published by Scholastic Inc.   Printed in the U.S.A.

ISBN-13: 978-0-545-50117-0
ISBN-10: 0-545-50117-2

Table of Contents

Table of Contents continued

Table of Contents continued

SCHOLASTIC

SYSTEM
44

NEXTGENERATION

Dear Student,

This book contains texts that are decodable. That means that most of the words used contain sound-spellings that you have learned.

It's easy to find the decodable texts that go with the *System 44* software. Just look at the Topic number printed at the top of each page or in the Table of Contents. Your teacher may ask you to read texts that go with lessons he or she is teaching.

Tips for Reading and Enjoying the Texts

- **Use what you know.** Try to sound out new words. Look for word parts you know. Break longer words into syllables. That will make them easier to read.

- **Think about what you read.** Retell or summarize the big ideas in the texts. This will help you understand what you read. Reread any parts of the text that confuse you.

- **Get help with word meaning.** Use the Glossary at the back of this book to find pronunciations and meanings for important words. Ask your teacher, a classmate, or a family member for help when you need to.

There are many types of texts in this book. They include short fiction, nonfiction, comics, text messages, emails, and more. Find out which most interest you. And, most of all, enjoy reading!

Sincerely,

Ivan

① Sam

I **am** Sam!   **Am** I Sam?   I **am**!

Word Count: 8

② Text Message

Msg

R U OK?

I **am** OK

I **am** 2!

Word Count: 9

To the Teacher: *Preteach short a and the word I before students read these passages.*

Decodable Digest

❶ Sssssnake!

❷ Stan's Bad Day

To the Teacher: *Preteach short a and the word I before students read these passages.*

1 Get Up, Nat!

2 Stan's Day

Stan **sat at** 5 A.M.

Stan **sat at** 9 A.M.

Stan **sat at** 8 P.M.?

Word Count: 15

❶ Nan Tricks Ann (Part 1)

Word Count:11

❷ Nan Tricks Ann (Part 2)

At 8:00 P.M.

Word Count:6

To the Teacher: *Preteach the word a and short a before students read these passages.*

Comics

1 Ant and Man?

A **tan mat**

An ant

A **man**

A **man! An ant!**
A **tan mat!**

Word Count: 15

2 A Man

A **man sat.**

A **man sat.**

A **man sat** and
sat.

A **man sat.**

Word Count: 14

1 Sap on a Cap!

A tan **cap**

A **pan** of **sap**

A tan **cap**!
A **pan** of **sap**!

A tan **cap**!
A **tap**! A **tap**!

Word Count: 21

2 A Map Nap?

Move, cat!

Nan **pats** Sam,
a tan cat.

Nan sat at a
map.

Sam naps.

Nan **taps** Sam!
"Sam, my **map!**"

Word Count: 21

To the Teacher: *Preteach the words* I *and* a *before students read these passages.*

c as in cat

❶ Cat Spat

Pat, a tan **cat,** naps on a mat.

Sam, a **cat,** taps Pat. Tap! Tap! Tap!

Sam, **can** Pat nap?

Word Count: 20

❷ At Camp Sacnac

Ann –
I am at **Camp** Sacnac!
I got tan at **camp.**
Can you send a **cap**
and some pants?
💜 Cam

Ann Capp
5 Pappas Ct.
Canton, CT 06109

42 USA

Word Count: 28

❶ Nat and a Cab

Nat ran at a **cab.**
Nat sat.

Bam! Bam! Bam!

Nat sat on a **cab!**

Word Count: 15

❷ Brant at Bat

Brant is at **bat.** Brant is at a mat. Brant pats a tan cap. Brant taps a **bat.** Brant taps a mat. Brant can **bat!**

Word Count: 25

To the Teacher: _Preteach the word_ a _before students read these passages._

❶ Pam, a Cat, a Rat, and a Bat

A cat can  a **rat**,

A **rat** can 👁 Pam.

Pam can 👁 a bat,

Can a bat 👁 them?

Word Count: 21

❷ No Rest for a Rat

A **rat** naps.

A cat! A **rat**!

A **rat** can't nap.

Word Count: 11

Poem

1 A Band Jams

Sam **taps cans.**

Nat **taps pans.**

Pat **snaps.**

Tad **raps.**

A band!

Word Count: 12

Comic

2 Sam's Maps

A map

Sam **scans maps.**

Sam **stamps maps.**

Sam **camps** with **maps.**

Word Count: 12

How can a map help you camp?

List

❶ Bill's Packing List

A List

- ☑ a bat
- ☑ a **mitt**
- ☑ tan pants
- ☑ a cap
- ☑ Pam's **pic**

Word Count: 12

Comic

❷ Homework Fibs?

A cat sat **in it!**   I am sick **in** bed.   A man ran at **it.**   **It** has a **rip in it!**

Word Count: 21

 Which fib is the hardest to believe? Tell why.

d as in _dog

1 Dad and Dibs

Dibs is my cat. Dibs bit Dad and ran! **Bad** cat!

Dad was **mad.** Dad ran, and so **did** Dibs, the bad cat!

Word Count: 23

2 The Bad Rap on Bats

It is **sad.** A bat has a **bad, bad** rap. A bat can nap in the day. And a bat can get **rid** of **bad** pests! Is a bat **bad?**

Are you **mad** at a bat's **bad** rap? Are you a bat fan?

Word Count: 43

 Write one fact about bats.

Fiction

❶ Fans for Sale

Fran has "**Fan**-tastic!" "**Fan**-tastic!" has **fans.** Fran ran a bad ad. Fran's ad has a bad, bad mistake. Fran is sad and Fran is mad! Fran has a **fit!** Is it Fran's last ad?

100%??? **Fans** are 10% off!

Word Count: 43

Fiction

❷ Fast Fins

Tim straps on **fins.**

He dips in!

He taps a crab.

The crab is mad!

Tim can swim **fast!**

Word Count: 21

Scram, crab!

 How do the fins help Tim?

h as in *hat*

❶ Ham in a Can?

This is in Kim's bag? A **ham** in a can and mints in a tin? Can Kim skip this? It is bad!

Word Count: 22

❷ Frank's Big Hit

Frank is at bat. Frank **hits** the ball. Frank **hits** it fast. Frank **hits** it home!

A fan in the stands tips his **hat.** "I am a fan! The kid is fast!"

Word Count: 32

 What sport does Frank play?

❶ Kip's Kit

Kip is a **kid.** Kip has a **kit.**

Kip did his **kit.**

Is Kip's **kit** bad?

His **kit** is bad!

Word Count: 23

❷ Kam's Pants

Kam has tan pants. The pants have a rip. Kam has a **kit.** The **kit** has pins. The **kit** has thread. Kam fixes the rip in his pants.

Word Count: 28

 What have you fixed? Tell about it.

❶ Top Mop Hits the Spot!

Got **spots?** You **cannot** miss the **spots** with this **mop!**

- ✔ An ink **dot?**
- ✔ Sand bits?
- ✔ Hand prints?

It is OK! It is **not** bad! The E-Z **Mop** can **top** any **mop!**

Word Count: 34

❷ Dot and Spot

Dot is Todd's cat. Dot is **not** fit. In fact, Dot is fat. And Dot naps a **lot.**

Todd got Spot. Spot is fit and fast! Spot chases Dot **nonstop.** Dot is mad at Spot. Dot is **not** fast!

Word Count: 39

 Why does Spot chase Dot?

Fiction

① Late at the Lab

Bill is at his **lab.** Bill **lifts** a kit. It tips! Bill drops the kit. The **lid** on the kit pops!

Now Bill must stop and mop the spill. Poor Bill!

Word Count: 31

List

② Lil's List

Lil has a long **list**. This is Lil's **list:**

- ✔ ham in a tin can
- ✔ a pot and a **lid**
- ✔ milk
- ✔ a mop

Can Lil fit it all in a box?

Word Count: 30

 Write one thing on Lil's list.

Comic

1 Rod and His Sax

Rod has to **fix** his **sax** at **six.** Rod drops his **sax** in a **box** and flips the lid.

Rod runs at a cab. Rod drops his **sax!**

A cab hits it! Rod is mad!

Can he **fix** his **sax** now?

Word Count: 43

Fiction

2 Ann and Max

Ann and Max are in the lab. Max has a hot pan. Ann adds a **box** of milk. Then, 1, 2, 3, 4, 5, **Six!** BAM!

Oops! Can Max and Ann **fix** this?

Word Count: 35

 Tell one thing people do in labs.

❶ Yackity Yack!

Max **packs** six fat **tack sacks.**

Kids in **socks kick rocks** on **docks.**

Word Count: 13

Fiction

❷ Stinky Socks

Rick sniffs his **socks.** His **socks** stink! In fact, his **socks** make him **sick!** Tim **picks** up Rick's **socks. Ick!** Tim **kicks** Rick's **socks!** Now Rick is not **sick,** and he is not mad at Tim.

"My **socks!**"

Word Count: 38

 What is Rick's problem? How does Tim fix it?

Fiction

❶ Slippery Stan

Stan sits on a **slick** rock. Stan **spots** a fat fish. He licks his lips.

Stan **stands** on the rock and **slips!** He cannot **stop!** Now, Stan is a **slick,** wet cat!

Word Count: 32

Fiction

❷ Colin the Slob

Colin is a **slob!** He **spits** his gum on his desk! He **spills** milk on his **stack** of disks. His socks **stick** on his fan! And Colin's socks **stink!** Colin has to **stop!**

Word Count: 34

What advice would you give to Colin?

Fiction

① All-U-Can-Fit Tent

Kim packs her **tent** in a **red** backpack. Look at Kim's **tent!** The **tent** is big! Kim can fit a **bed** in the **tent!**

Kim thinks, "It is sad that I cannot fit a **bed** in this **red** backpack."

Word Count: 39

Fiction

② Which Sled Wins?

The **sled** race is on! Six **men** in black tops sit on a black **sled.** The black **sled** is fast.

Ten men in **red** tops sit on a **red sled.** The **red sled** is fast. But it is not big. Can the **ten men** fit? Can the **red sled** win? The black **sled** hits a rock! The **red sled** wins!

Word Count: 60

 Why did the red sled win?

j as in jet

① Jen Jets!

Jen is a **jock.** Jen met Jin on a run.

Jin asks to wed Jen.

Jen cannot wed yet. Jen is in a **jam.** Jen **jets!**

Word Count: 26

② Jed's Jam

Jed is in a cab. Jed's cab is in a bad traffic **jam.** His cab stops. It has no gas left in it. Jed can fix this! Jed can jog to his **job!**

Word Count: 34

 Why did Jed's cab stop?

❶ The Web

The **Web** is not bad! It has a lot of facts. The **Web** has facts on **wax,** jets, pets, and rocks. It can show you jobs, maps, and stocks.

But a lot of **Web** facts can be bad. It is best to stop and check the facts you spot on the **Web.**

Word Count: 52

❷ Cat in a Well

A sad cat is in a bad jam. It fell in a **well.** The **well** is dim. It is **wet** and slick. The **well** is 24-feet deep. The cat **went** 10 feet in the **well.** Then it slid! The cat cannot hop back to the **well's** rim. The cat is mad! It has sat in the dim **well** for six hours! Help!

Word Count: 63

  How deep is the well?

❶ Tuck and the Tub

Brad has Tuck. Tuck is **just** a **pup.** Tuck **runs** in the **mud.** Yuck! Brad fills the **tub.** Tuck **jumps** in the **suds.** "Stop it, Tuck!"

Word Count: 26

❷ Sunny Side Up

Todd and Wen get **up** at six. Todd wants flapjacks, ham, and a **cup** of milk. **But** Wen **just** wants a **muffin.**

Todd and Wen hop on a **bus,** and head to the **Truck** Stop Inn. They are in **luck!** It has **stuff** that hits the spot!

Word Count: 50

 What does Todd want for breakfast?

Fiction

① Got Ya!

Jack and his pals step out to play **tag.**

"Not It!" yells Jack.

"Not It," yell Lin, Alex, and Jen.

Sol is "It." Sol can run fast. He **tags** Jen. Now Jen is "It." Jen is slick. She is fast. She **tags** Tim. Tim's **legs** are tired. Tim cannot **jog.** Tim has to sit.

"I must quit!" yells Tim. Word Count: 59

Fiction

② Peg and the Bug

Gil **jogs** with his **big dog,** Peg. Peg **digs** up **bugs.** Gil yells if Peg brings a **bug** back. Yuck! "Peg, **get** rid of that **bug!**" Gil will not let Peg on his bed. He pushes her off. Peg and the **bug** must nap on the **rug!**

Word Count: 47

 Why won't Gil let Peg on his bed?

① Say Yes!

YASMIN'S TAG SALE

Yes, you can get the best for less! I sell rock and hip-hop CDs, lots of wigs, cups and mugs, a rare **yak** pendant, a big red and black rug, and more!

Yet, that is not it! I sell **yams**, figs, and plums as well. **Yum**!

☞ **2:00 at 5 Yell Back Rd.**

Word Count: 55

Advice

② Yuck!

Dear Kim,

Help! Mom tells me, "Eat **yams.**" But yams are **yuck, yuck, yuck!** If I **yell,** "Mom, I hate **yams,**" Mom gets mad. **Yet,** if I say **"Yes!,"** I get sick! Kim, I cannot win! What can I do?

— Yan

Word Count: 41

 What should Yan do?

① Man With a Van

Fast Frank can help you with any job!

☑ Need a **van**?
☑ Stuck in the mud?
☑ Can not lift a box?
☑ Run out of gas?
☑ Bring a cat to the **vet**?
☑ Mend a rip in a **vest**?

You are in luck! I am
the man for the job!
Call Fast Frank,
The Man With a **Van!**

Fast Frank (555) 515–5555

Word Count: 60

Fiction

② A Trip to the Vet

Val's dog, Socks, is sick. She will not eat. She just naps on a quilt. Val takes Socks in a **van** to **visit** the **vet.** The **vet** gets a pill from his **vest** and hands it to Socks.

The dog pill helps! Socks gets up. She runs to Val and wags. Socks wants a snack! Val is glad!

Word Count: 58

 How does Socks get well?

① Zeb's Gift

Rick naps a lot and has no **zest.** He is sick.

Quick! Get in the van!

Zeb grabs his pals. They **zip** by Rick's with a gift.

Get well quick, Rick!

Word Count: 31

② Zip Up the Bucks!

Scott stuck ten bucks in his tan backpack. **"Zip** that up, Scott," said Ellen. "I cannot **zip** it. The zipper is stuck."

"Quick, let me help," said Ellen. "OK, it **zips!"**

"Ellen, you are the best!"

Word Count: 37

 What is wrong with Scott's backpack?

Fiction

1 Quack!

Quinn and I were in my van. Ten ducks sat in the lot. "**Quack, quack, quack!**" went the ducks. The ducks would not **quit.**

"Quinn, I cannot back up!" I said.

Quinn let out a big "**QUACK!**" The ducks ran to the grass. "**Quick,**" Quinn said. "You can back up." Word Count: 50

Fiction

2 The Pop Quiz

"There will be a **quick quiz** in class. It is a pop **quiz,**" said Miss Ban.

"But you did not tell us about the **quiz!**"

"It is just a **quick quiz** on rocks," she said.

Rocks? Jon is in luck. He has a lot of rocks. Jon got an A on the **quiz!**

Word Count: 53

 What kind of quiz did Miss Ban give?

❶ Pat Scans the Ads

Pat has to get a job fast. She **scans** the ads. Pat **spots** a job with a vet. But Pat does not like pets. Next, Pat **spots** a desk job. But Pat does not like to sit **still.** Last, Pat sees a job on TV. Pat loves TV! But can she act?

Word Count: 52

 What job do you want? Tell about it.

❷ Skipping Snacks

Scott was in a big, big rush. Scott had to **skip** his **snack.**

At his game, Scott felt sick. He did not run. He did not jump. He felt bad!

Scott said, "Next time, I will not **skip** a **snack!**"

Word Count: 40

Fiction

① Bill's Boss

Bill does not like his job. His **boss,** Ann, gets mad a lot. Ann **yells** at the **staff.**

Bill quits his job. At his next job, Bill is the **boss.** Will he **yell?** Time will **tell!**

Word Count: 36

Science Nonfiction

② Shake, Rattle, and Buzz

A snake **will** bask in the sun on hot rocks and **cliffs.** It **will** sit on the sand and in **grass** as **well.** It **will** make a **fuss** to **tell** you to back **off.** As a **bluff,** it can **hiss** and **puff** up.

A rattlesnake has a tail that **will buzz** and rattle. If you hear a buzz, do not panic and **yell.** Just get past it fast!

Word Count: 68

 What should you do if you see a snake?

❶ Stan's Quest

Stan went to get a pen in his **desk.** He found a big black and red bug in his **desk** instead. That bug had lots of legs!

Stan is now on a **quest.** His **task** is to get rid of the **pests** in his house. Stan will not **rest** a bit until he zaps every **last** bug!

Word Count: 57

 What does Stan find in his desk?

❷ A Strong Wind

This **gust** of wind is too **brisk!** Do not **risk** it! Quick! Run in **fast!**

What a mess! Let's grab plastic bags and pick it up.

Word Count: 26

❶ Justin's Handheld

Justin just got a brand new **handheld** device. He got it in a **contest.** Justin can text and send messages to his pals.

Justin's **handheld** is so **compact.** It fits in his **jacket pocket!**

Justin sends a **comment** to his pal, Robin. "Man, this is slick!" Word Count: 46

❷ Denim

Denim is a **fabric. Jackets,** tops, hats, pants, and bags can be **denim. Denim** can come in black, blue, red, and tan. **Denim** tends not to rip fast as well. **Denim** is a fantastic **fabric!** It has lots of uses!

Word Count: 40

 What can be made of denim?

Life Skills Nonfiction

❶ Blog Tips

What is a **blog?** You can **click** to get to a **blog** on the Web. In fact, **"blog"** stands for "Web log." A **blog** is a log kept on the Web. A **blog** can be on lots of fun topics. You can **blab** on a band, a **class,** a pet—whatever!

If you get a **blog,** just tell stuff you would be **glad** to tell Mom and Dad. Anyone on the Web can read it!

Word Count: 75

Blog

❷ Our Camp Blog

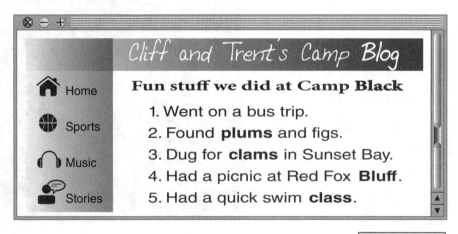

Cliff and Trent's Camp Blog

🏠 Home
🏀 Sports
🎧 Music
💬 Stories

Fun stuff we did at Camp Black

1. Went on a bus trip.
2. Found **plums** and figs.
3. Dug for **clams** in Sunset Bay.
4. Had a picnic at Red Fox **Bluff**.
5. Had a quick swim **class**.

Word Count: 43

What would you write a blog about? Tell about it.

❶ The Frilly Hat

Granddad picks up a lot of odd stuff in junk shops. And then he sends it to me! I just got a hat as a gift. The hat is tan. It has a big **brim** with red velvet pompoms stuck on it. And the **brim** has **frills** as well. Yuck! What was Granddad thinking?!

Word Count: 54

 Tell about the worst gift you ever got.

❷ Crazy Cuts

Cam: I must get my hair cut. It's puffy on top and has lots of **frizz.** I cannot fix it. I am sick of it. Should I get a buzz cut and **crop** it all off? Can you help me pick a cut?

Cass: Not a problem. Let me at it!

Word Count: 51

Fiction

1 Cat Tricks

Kim and Lin go on a picnic. Kim packs a snack and a **blanket.** They bring Lin's cat, Fluff, as well.

After the snack, Lin asks, "Where is Fluff?"

Kim and Lin cannot spot her!

"Is Fluff on the **blanket?"** Lin asks.

"Did she run away?" Kim asks. "No, I spot Fluff's **tracks,"** says Lin.

The **tracks** end at the picnic basket! Fluff is in the basket!

Word Count: 67

News Article

2 A Big Plan

Man Plans to Win Truck

TRENT, MASS.— Trent **Trucks** is having a big contest. The prize is a brand-new red **truck**. The odds are slim, but local man Sam Speck **plans** to win. "I will win that **truck**," Speck said to reporters. To get the **truck,** Speck has to win a six-mile run. The run is in ten weeks. "I can win it," Speck said. "I have a **plan.** I will run at a track. I will get fit. I will get fast. I will not quit! **Trust** me, I can do it!"

Word Count: 95

 How does Sam plan to win?

Fiction

① The Grill Is Hot!

I **grab** a rib from the **grill.** It is still hot. It is too hot! I let it **drop. Splat!**

I better **scrub** it up before Mom gets back! This is **grim.** Mom will get upset if she sees that big **black** and red spot on her rug.

Word Count: 48

Fiction

② Drums Rock!

Granddad got Greg a **drum** set as a gift. But Greg's dad is **strict.** He will not let Greg keep it. Greg's dad cannot stand the racket. But Greg's mom has a **plan.**

"Greg, you can get an air guitar instead," she says with a **grin.**

Mom **strums** a bit. Greg just gets mad at his mom's bad plan. Greg **grabs** his **drumsticks** and stomps out!   Word Count: 66

 Tell why Greg's dad would not let him keep his drum set.

❶ The Gift

Dear Get **Help,**

   I made a glass **lamp** in my **craft** class. I **left** it with Jed as a **gift,** but I want it back. I am sad. Jed will not give the glass **lamp** back. Is Jed a bad friend?

Mad at Jed

Dear Mad at Jed,

   A **gift** is a **gift**. You cannot **expect** Jed to just hand the glass **lamp** back. Get past it and make a new glass **lamp!**

Get **Help**

Word Count: 75

❷ Win With Robin's Help

Travis: Robin Cross has **left** her **stamp** on tennis. In **fact,** Robin has won seven medals. Robin, what helps you win?

Robin: I am **swift,** and I have a **gift** for tennis.

Travis: Can we **expect** a win at your next tennis match?

Robin: Yes, I intend to win. You can bet on it!

Travis: Any tips?

Robin: If you can, visit a tennis **camp.** A tennis **camp** will **help** expand your skills!

Word Count: 73

What sport would you like to be good at?

Email

❶ Frank's Spring Trip

From: Frank Baskin

To: Sang Son

Subject: My **Spring** Trip

Sang,

I just got back from my **spring** trip! I went with my mom and dad. It was a blast!

At first, I was mad! I slipped on a wet rock and slid down a mud **bank**. And a **skunk** got in my tent—and the tent still **stinks**! I also got a bug **sting** on my back. :-(But then, I had a lot of fun. I got to **drink** from a crisp **spring**. And I went on a raft trip. I even spotted a fox and its cubs in a den.

The trip was a blast!

Frank

Word Count: 108

How-To

❷ Art From Junk!

Make a Mobile: A Quick and Fun Craft Project!

❶ Get string, tin cans, and lots of **junk**—stuff like plastic **rings**, rocks, and strips of fabric.

❷ Glue the **junk** on the tin cans.

❸ Next, **hang** the cans on **strings**.

❹ **Hang** the **strings** on a hanger.

❺ **Hang** it up!

Word Count: 48

❶ Drastic Measures

It is 7:00 and Jeff has a basketball **ticket** in his **pocket.** His **ticket** is for a **fantastic** spot in the front row. It cost Jeff a **hundred** bucks!

Jeff has to get there fast! He gets in a cab, but his cab gets stuck in **traffic!** Jeff has his cab stop and he gets out. "This is **drastic,**" Jeff says. He runs **seven** blocks. But Jeff is in luck! He gets there just in time to see a **fantastic** three-point **basket!**

Word Count: 83

 Why is Jeff running?

❷ Fantastic Deals

Hot Deals on **Fantastic** Trips!

Jump on a tram and **visit** San Francisco's best spots!

- Step back in time and visit the Mission **District**
- Stop off at the **public** markets
- Have a **picnic** in the **Sunset District**
- **Visit** the inns in Nob Hill

Get **tickets** at
555-6780
(Tickets subject to tax)

Word Count: 52

Poem

❶ Grass in the Wind

Next to a still **pond**,

a **strand** of grass **bends** and shifts

in a swift soft **wind**.

Word Count: 17

News Article

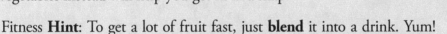

❷ Fitness Hints

Get Fit!

by Trent Hand

Think you cannot get fit? Well, you can! It is a fact. Just two habits can **send** you on a fantastic **and** fast track to fitness!

- Habit 1: Cut back on junk food and soft drinks. This stuff is bad, **and** has a lot of calories. Eating fruits **and** vegetables instead will help you get fit in a snap.

  Fitness **Hint**: To get a lot of fruit fast, just **blend** it into a drink. Yum!

- Habit 2: Get lots of exercise! Just walk, skip, run, **bend**, twist, and jump for 30 minutes a day. If you can, it is best to **stand** and not sit. Go for a long jog. See if you can **sprint** fast.

  Fitness **Hint**: Get fitness pals. A fitness plan can help you **bond** with a friend, **and** Mom **and** Dad as well!

Word Count: 142

 Do you have a plan for keeping fit? Tell about it.

Comic

❶ Trip Snapshots

My best friend Tess and I went on a fantastic trip to the Florida wetlands last spring. I got lots and lots of **snapshots.**

This **snapshot** is best. It is a **shot** of Tess and me at sunset. That is a **fishing** boat in back. Tess and I ate lots of **fresh fish** and crabs.

This **shot** is of us standing in grass at Big Gum Swamp. We had a blast on the trip. I **wish** I could go back.

Word Count: 80

Note

❷ Rush, Josh!

Josh,

   Granddad needs you to cut his grass. His grass is so long, it is up to his **shins**. And Granddad will give you ten bucks if you **finish** the job fast. His lawnmower is in the **shed** in back. The red gas can is next to it. And the key is in a tin can on the top left **shelf**. Josh, please **rush**! No napping until Granddad's grass is cut.

Mom

Word Count: 72

 What does Josh's mom want him to do?

Science Nonfiction

❶ Chimps at Risk

Chimps can help us a lot. In fact, in 1961, a **chimp** went up to space in a rocket. That **chimp** was a fantastic animal.

But **chimps** are at risk. It is sad. Hunting is a big risk to **chimps.** A **chimp** should not be taken from its habitat, but some **chimps** are kept as pets. This must end. We must take steps to stop **such** bad acts. It is best to let **chimps** exist in peace. We must help **chimps!**

Word Count: 81

Fiction

❷ Chuck's Laptop

Chuck just got a laptop from his dad. He can do lots of tasks on his laptop. Chuck can do his homework on his laptop. Chuck can **chat,** shop, and **check** his email as well. On the Web, Chuck can play **chess.** Chuck is glad his laptop can do so **much!**

Word Count: 51

What does Chuck do on his laptop?

① Catch Some Fun!

Spend a Fantastic Day at Club Shellfish!

Club Shellfish is brand new! It the best hot spot in town!

- Swim and **catch** a wave.
- Have a dish of fresh clams and a **batch** of shrimp at lunch.

- Hunt for shells and visit the best shops.
- **Catch** a fish off the dock.
- Or just **stretch** on the rich sand.

Visit Club Shellfish Today!

415 Black Sand Rd. 555-SHEL (7435)

Word Count: 69

② Fetch, Mitch, Fetch!

My dog, Mitch, is such a fantastic dog! My friends and I crack up at his tricks. Mitch can do the usual dog stuff. He can **catch** a ball and **fetch** a stick. Mitch can sit up and beg for snacks.

But Mitch can do the best trick! If I yell, "Mitch, give Ted a kiss," Mitch will **stretch** up to Ted's chest and lick his chin! Ted looks mad for a bit, but then he just laughs. Mitch is the best!

Word Count: 82

 What tricks can Mitch do?

❶ Dish Trouble

Dear Meg,

I have a job. I scrub houses. I dust, mop, and pick up stuff. But, last week, I got a **dish** off a **shelf** to dust. I tried to **catch** the **dish,** but I did not get it. In a **flash,** it broke into a hundred bits! I had to drop the bits in the **trash.** I cannot pay for it. I do not have **much cash.** I am not **rich.** Can I just quit? Help!

Jen in a Jam

Dear Jen in a Jam,

Do not quit. It is just a **dish.** And we all drop a **dish** sometimes. Have a **chat** with your boss. She can help. It is best just to tell.

Meg

Word Count: 118

Science Nonfiction

❷ Fresh Water Life

A pond is an area of **fresh,** still water. A pond is not as big as a lake. A pond habitat is **rich** with plants and animals. You can spot a **bunch** of frogs at a pond. You can even spot **fish** and insects that live in ponds as well. Plants, **such** as long grasses and **rushes,** grow in a pond and on its bank.

If you visit a pond, sit still and see what plants and animals you can spot. Word Count: 81

 What can you spot at a pond?

❶ Classes For All!

Fantastic Spring **Classes!**

- "Classic Comic **Sketches**"
- "Baseball: Hits and **Pitches**"
- "Fast Knitting **Stitches**"
- "Blogs 101"
- "Baskets from **Branches**"
- "Hot Jobs for Kids"

Pick from 50 **classes** at Westland College.
Tell a friend and get $50 back!

Word Count: 36

❷ Buzz Smashes All Records!

Buzz will impress you. Buzz is as strong as an ox. Buzz can bench-press 300 pounds!

Buzz has a strong, fast pitch. His **pitches** stun players.

At tennis **matches,** Buzz **smashes** tennis balls with his racket!

Once, Buzz had to get ten **stitches.** He did not flinch a bit. Buzz is so strong!

Word Count: 58

 What sports does Buzz play?

❶ Thick Fog Wrecks Ship

Seth: Sam, check out **this** snapshot in today's paper. A big ship got stuck on some rocks off the Gulf.

Sam: I saw it, Seth. How did a ship end up on the rocks?

Seth: I **think** the **thick** fog hid the rocks. **Then** the ship struck **them.**

Sam: I bet the ship's crew got a big shock when the ship hit.

Seth: Yes, but I bet it was a bigger shock to the rocks!

Word Count: 75

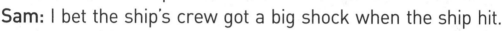

❷ Rings and Things

Advice

Dear Meg,

Help! I **think** I lost Mom's best rings! I just tried **them** on once, but now I cannot find **them**! Must I tell Mom? If Mom gets mad, **then** she will not let me go to Thad's party! **This** is bad!

In Distress

Dear In Distress,

That is sad, but you must tell Mom. **Then**, you and Mom can hunt for the rings. If you two cannot spot **them, then** you and Mom can discuss a plan to get her new rings.

Meg

Word Count: 85

What problem does Meg solve?

Fiction

❶ No Math for Kat

Kat had **chills** and did not feel well. She left school early. Kat's mom felt her forehead. It felt hot.

"Am I sick?" Kat asked.

"Yes. Just get in bed," said Kat's mom. "Rest **this** wet **cloth** on your forehead. I will bring you hot **chicken broth."**

"But I must **finish** my **math,"** Kat said.

"Get a lot of rest, and **then** you can **finish** your **math,"** said Kat's mom. Word Count: 70

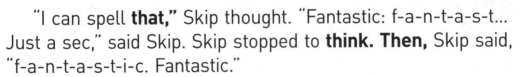

Fiction

❷ Spelling Champ!

Skip Ash held his breath. He thought, "Just one last word! If I spell it, I will win the big contest!" The Ashes win lots of contests—but not Skip. His twin, Rob, wins big **math** contests. Alex, a tennis nut, wins tennis **matches.** Skip just had to win this!

The man looked at Skip and said, "Spell 'fantastic.'"

"I can spell **that,"** Skip thought. "Fantastic: f-a-n-t-a-s-t... Just a sec," said Skip. Skip stopped to **think. Then,** Skip said, "f-a-n-t-a-s-t-i-c. Fantastic."

The man nodded at Skip. "Yes! You are the spelling **champ!"**

Word Count: 92

What word does Skip spell? Does he get it right?

❶ Cash In on Cleaning Up

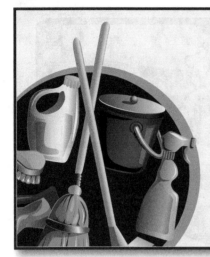

If you like...

- **dusting** benches and desks
- **mopping** up bad spills
- **polishing** brass until it shines
- **stitching** up snags in socks
- **picking** up lots of stuff
- making lots of cash

Then I have a job just for you!
Contact Dust Busters at 555-DUST. Ask for Kim.

Word Count: 47

❷ Just Checking In

Dialogue

Ann: Did you and Frank have a fun **camping** trip?

Beth: Yes, it was fantastic. But it was a quick trip! I spent much of it **sketching** the beautiful landscape and **visiting** with pals.

fishing, resting...

Frank spent much of the trip **fishing** off the back of a raft. And he spent the last day just **resting** in his tent!

Ann: Fishing? Resting? Sketching? Visiting pals? I wish I had come on the trip!

Word Count: 74

What did Frank do on the trip?

Decodable Digest **57**

Comic

❶ Just What Dad Wanted!

Dad got a brand new job. Dad **hinted** that he wanted a gift.

Mom said that Dad could pick his gift. Dad could get a chess set, a set of golf clubs, a laptop, or a big TV.

Guess what Dad **ended** up with!

Word Count: 44

Fiction

❷ The Spotted Steps

I got a job last spring. I had to fix Mr. Smith's steps. I **sanded** and swept them. Next, I painted them red. Then I **planted** flowers next to them.

But the next day, I got a big shock! When I went back to Mr. Smith's, the steps were **spotted** with footprints! I was mad!

Word Count: 57

 What happened to the steps?

Fiction

❶ As the Clock Ticked...

The Ducks had to get a basket, but the clock **ticked** fast! Quentin West **rushed** up next to the basket, but the Frogs **blocked** his shot. Quentin **passed** Fred King the ball. Then Fred **jumped** up and **dunked** it! As the game **ended**, fans in the **packed** stands **yelled** and **clapped.** The Ducks were champs!

Word Count: 55

Fiction

❷ A Rushed Morning

What a morning! I did not hear my alarm clock and slept in. I got up at seven! Then, I **jumped** out of bed and **rushed** to get **dressed.** Next, I **filled** a glass with milk, **spilled** it, and **mopped** it up. I **packed** a lunch in a snap, but lost it when the bag **ripped.** Then I **dashed** to catch the bus. But I just **missed** it and got to class late. To top things off, I got **punished** for being late! What a bad day!

Word Count: 87

Why is he late for school? Write one reason.

Endings *-ing*, *-ed*

❶ Dishing With a Chef

Nell Smith: I am here **visiting** with chef Todd Janns. Todd, what is this dish?

Todd Janns: Nell, it's called "Fish Yum." I **invented** it. It has fresh fish, yams, nuts, and black figs in it. Will you test it?

Nell Smith: Todd, I love **testing** food, and I'm **expecting** that this dish will be **thrilling.**

Todd Janns: How is it?

Nell Smith: Well...it is **disgusting.** Next time, try it with no yams, nuts and figs.

Todd Janns: OK, Nell, thanks for **telling** it like it is. I will be **testing** all my dishes on you!

Word Count: 97

❷ Extending Time

Word Count: 58

➡ **If a "Time Extender" were real, how would you use it?**

Science Nonfiction

1 Desert Mammals

A desert is hot! And it gets less than 9.8 inches of rain a year. That is not much.

The **constant** sun and hot sand **affect** the **mammals** that live there. They must **adapt.** One **mammal** that has **adapted** is the camel. A camel's long lashes and long legs help protect it from the strong sun and hot sand.

Word Count: 59

Idioms

2 Instant Fun!

Check out this list of idioms and their meanings!

- Frank pressed the **pedal** to the **metal.** *Frank went fast.*
- Ben has a bone to pick. *Ben has a problem.*
- Can I level with you? *Can I just tell you the truth?*
- You bet! *Yes, no problem!*
- Can Jen lend a hand? *Can Jen help us?*
- Granddad is no spring chicken. *Granddad is getting old.*

Word Count: 64

 Think of an idiom. Write it down.

**Unstressed Closed
Syllables with *e* as in *camel*

Fiction

❶ A Fowl Problem!

Kim, I will **level** with you. I have a big **problem** with Bill's **chickens**. The clucking and scratching is constant. When the **chickens** spot me, they run at me in an instant. It's upsetting!

Until he gets rid of the **chickens**, I am not coming back to the ranch. It's me or the **chickens!**

Word Count: 54

Fiction

❷ Level 10

Jed loves games. He thinks the best one is Metal Max. Jed has to get to the top **level!** He is on **level seven.** But Jed must get to **level** ten.

The **problem** is that Mom and Dad think Jed plays Metal Max too much. I can see Jed has a lot of **talent.** But I think Mom and Dad could just be right!

Word Count: 64

 Are video games a waste of time? Give your opinion.

**Unstressed Closed
Syllables with *i* as in *tonsil***

Fiction

❶ Tonsil Trouble

I have felt sick for a long time. My throat is red and it stings. It is killing me! My doctor said I must check into the hospital and get my **tonsils** out. I am upset!

Mom insists that the hospital is not that bad. Granddad will visit and bring gifts. I can get a TV next to my bed. And I can suck on juice pops to chill my throat.

OK! I will admit that this **"tonsil** thing" is not so bad!

Word Count: 83

Fiction

❷ A Fossil Fortune?

My dog, Rocket, digs up a lot of stuff. He digs up sticks, rocks, and disgusting slugs. But Rocket also digs up my dad's plants. Rocket's digging makes Dad really mad.

Yesterday, Rocket dug up an odd object.

"Yuck! What is this?" I asked Dad.

"This is a **fossil!**" Dad said. "It is the skull of an **animal** from the past. It is a thrilling thing!"

For once, Dad was not mad at Rocket.   Word Count: 74

 What did Rocket find that made Dad happy?

Science Nonfiction

❶ The Grand Canyon

Wind and rain carved the Grand **Canyon** from rocks. It spans 8,000 feet from top to **bottom.** Lots of plants and animals are **common** to the **canyon.** It has 1,500 plant species, such as cactus, grasses, shrubs, and yuccas. It has 89 mammal species, such as foxes, bats, and elk. The Grand **Canyon** is a fun spot to visit. Word Count: 60

❷ Trip to the Canyon

Dialogue

Jasmin: Devon, let's get a mule to take us to the **canyon bottom.** It will be fun, and they do not cost much to rent.

Devon: Fun? Are you kidding? It will not be much fun if it **gallops** or bucks!

Jasmin: Devon, this is a **common** trip. People **seldom** get hurt.

Devon: Seldom? I think I will just check out the **canyon bottom** from that glass walkway on the west rim!

Word Count: 72

  Would you ride a mule to the bottom of the Grand Canyon? Tell why or why not.

❶ A Helpful Hand

The man in the big red house next door has a bad back problem. I try to act **helpful** to him. I pitch in if I can.

I help him pick up heavy stuff. I bring his trash out back to his big black trash can. And I have his keys so I can get in fast if he has a problem. I am glad that he is **trustful** of me. Sometimes he tells me that he is **thankful.** Then he tries to slip ten bucks in my back pocket. But I just hand it back with a big grin. It is just good to be a **helpful** friend. Word Count: 109

 In what ways are you helpful? List one or two ways.

❷ The Cat and the Cactus

I picked up a **cactus** plant in a plant shop. I set the **cactus** plant next to my bed. At the time, my cat, Muffin, napped on the bed. When Muffin got up, she saw the **cactus** plant. Muffin just had to inspect it! Muffin sniffed the **cactus** plant. Then Muffin brushed up against it! "Meow!" Now, Muffin will not go near that **cactus** plant! Word Count: 65

❶ An Incredible Tale

One day, Elton, an elephant, **stumbled** upon Trent, a **little** turtle. Trent was sitting in a **puddle.** In a flash, Elton picked up Trent with his trunk and tossed him! Trent landed in a shrub filled with **prickles.**

"What did I do?" asked Trent.

"You bit my trunk when we were **little!**" yelled Elton.

"**Impossible!** You cannot remember that!" Trent **trembled.**

"Yes I can," Elton **giggled.** "I have turtle recall." | Word Count: 70 |

❷ A Little Problem?

Dear Just Ask,

Help! I have a bad problem. I cannot **handle** my lab partner, Kevin! He is very timid! If Kevin has to talk with me, Kevin just **mumbles**. We had to discuss a lab in class, but Kevin just **trembled**. The whole class **giggled** at us! It is such a **struggle!** Thanks!

Fed Up

Dear Fed Up,

The answer is **simple!** Just make friends with Kevin. Ask him about himself. Compliment him. Win his trust. Be a pal and help him make friends in class. Then, Kevin will be confident. His shyness will **crumble.** Best wishes!

Just Ask

| Word Count: 100 |

 Tell two ways you could help a person be confident.

Interview

❶ Fantastic Travels

Shantel: I am just catching up with explorer Bob Mitchell. Bob, I hear your last trip had a few snags. Tell us about your **travels.**

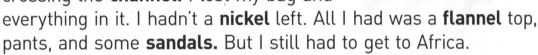

Bob: Well, my boat tipped just as I was crossing the **channel.** I lost my bag and everything in it. I hadn't a **nickel** left. All I had was a **flannel** top, pants, and some **sandals.** But I still had to get to Africa.

Shantel: What happened next? How did you get to Africa?

Bob: Well, with luck, I **signaled** a passing ship, and it picked me up. I got a job on the ship and got to Africa with a lot of cash!

Shantel: Bob, that is incredible!

Shantel: This is Shantel Smith for Channel 10! Back to you, Nick!

Word Count: 126

Schedule

❷ Channel Surfing

Channel	6:00–7:00
Animal Channel 🐕	• African **Mammals:** Facts about Black-Backed **Jackals** • **Kennel** Club Dog Show: Will the Basset or the Jack Russell Get the **Medal?**
Health **Channel** ➕	• **Dental** Tips: Brushing and Flossing Help • Get Fit: **Pedal** That Bike!
Travel Channel ✈	• Pack a **Duffel** Bag: Top-Notch Trips to England • **Sentimental Travels:** The Best Wedding Trips

 Which of these shows would you watch? Tell why.

Word Count: 66

Fiction

① The Game

Kevin, James, and Kristen played a baseball **game** with their class. Kristen pitched for her team.

Kristen pitched a fast ball to Kevin. He did not get the first pitch. But Kevin did get the second pitch. Kevin ran fast to first **base.**

Next up was James. James went up to the **plate.** James swung his bat at Kristen's pitch. James hit the pitch! It went spinning past Kristen. James hit a home run!

Kevin ran fast and crossed the **plate!** Then James crossed the **plate!** The score was 2 to 0. Kristen was not thrilled with this **game!**

Glossary Links
pitched
home run

Word Count: 99

 Who hit the home run?

2 Catch a Wave!

Want to have a lot of fun and get a big rush? Then you must give surfing a shot! Surfing is simple. It just **takes** a lot of practice. Stick with it and you will **tame** big **waves** in a flash.

To catch a **wave,** paddle out on a surfboard. The spot where you go to catch a **wave** is called the "**take-**off zone."

If you spot a big **wave,** jump up fast! This is called the "pop-up." Do not **hesitate** as you pop up. That will **make** you crash in an instant. Then, just stand up and travel with the **wave.** This is called "catching a **wave,"** and it is a big thrill.

Glossary Links
paddle
surfboard

When your skills are top notch, hang your toes from the rim of the surfboard. This is a "hang ten." Surf's up!

Word Count: 138

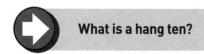
What is a hang ten?

Science Nonfiction

❶ Vines Alive

A **vine** is a plant that has long, thin stems. The **vines'** stems, or tendrils, can grab and attach on things such as sticks.

A tendril will shift toward an object that brushes against it. Then, a tendril will twist around that object and cling to it.

Lots of **vines** cling to bricks and the **sides** of buildings. **Vines** can grow in the shade and in the sun as well.

Ivy is an example of a common **vine**. Ivy has flat, green leaves that **shine**.

Grapes, peanuts, and pumpkins grow on **vines**. And **ripe** grapes off the **vine** can make fantastic jams.

Word Count: 102

Glossary Links
tendrils
object

 Tell two things that grow on a vine.

❷ Free Time

○ ○ ○

✉ ✉ ✉ 🗑

From: Trish Rust

To: Mike Hines

Subject: I **like**...

Pen Pal Mike,

This is what I **like** to do in my free **time:**

- Chill out with classmates (I **like** this best!)
- Run **five miles (Yikes!)**
- Skate at the rink
- Play drums in my rock band
- Make wax candles
- Take catnaps
- Swim and **dive** at the pool on **Pine** Cone **Drive**
- Collect stamps
- Fly **kites**
- Shop for rap, pop, and rock CDs
- **Ride bikes** with Jane

Tell me what you **like** to do in your free **time.**

Trish

Word Count: 87

Glossary Links
chill out
rink

What do you like to do in your free time?
Write two or three things.

❶ Facts About Snakes

Snakes can be found in lots of spots, but not where it is cold. A **snake** is a legless **reptile** that has **scales** on its skin.

Scales protect a **snake's** body. The **scales** help a **snake** grip the ground as it **slides**. A **snake's scales** do not grow as the **snake** grows. When its **scales** do not fit, a snake sheds its skin.

Snakes like to **dine** on insects, eggs, and rats. A **snake** smells with its tongue. This helps it catch its food. When a **snake strikes** or **bites** its victim, its fangs inject venom into its prey.

Glossary Links
venom
prey

Snakes have gotten a bad **name**. Lots of people think **snakes** are bad. But **snakes** are not.

Just be **wise**! If you do not bug a **snake**, it will not **bite** you!

Word Count: 131

 List four things you learned about snakes.

❷ The Tale of the Lion and the Fox

Once upon a **time,** Lion said with a **smile,** "I have a bad illness." Lots of animals visited him at his **cave** to wish him well. But, as soon as the animals went in his den, Lion **ate** them up.

Fox, a quick-thinking animal, saw that lots of animals had vanished. Fox suspected that Lion had eaten them. Fox went to Lion and asked him, "How is everything?"

In a sad voice Lion said, "I am not well, Fox. In fact, I do not think that I have much **time** left. Step in and visit a bit."

"Thanks, but I will not come in for a visit," said Fox. "You cannot trick me. I can tell that lots of animals went in your **cave,** but none **came** back out."

Word Count: 130

Glossary Links
vanished
suspected

 What is the moral, or lesson, of this story?

Profile

1 The Ice Dive

Would you dive in **ice**-cold water? This incredible Dutch man did. Wim Hof likes to do **ice** stunts. In fact, his nickname is the "**Ice** Man."

In 2002, Hof traveled to a lake in Finland. He drilled two big rectangles in the **ice.** The rectangles were 54 meters apart. That is not quite 190 feet. Hof then swam under the **ice** and **raced** to the finish line. Hof set a record with his **race** time.

That's quite a **nice** dive!

Word Count: 81

Glossary Links
incredible
record

 How did Wim Hof set a record?

❷ BMX Bikes Race Fast!

If you get a **chance,** you should attend a BMX bike **race.** BMX stands for *bicycle motocross.*

In BMX **races,** riders **race** down a hill as fast as their bikes will take them. Whoever gets the fastest time wins a **nice** prize. The best BMX bike racers must have the strength, quickness, and bike-handling skills it takes to win.

It is quite a thrill watching BMX riders do tricks on ramps. They can do stunts like spins and backflips in which their bikes rise up over the top of a ramp.

BMX bikes are **nice** bikes for speed. They are not as big as other bikes, but must have thick tires and a strong frame. Next time you crave a thrilling trip, get to a BMX bike **race!**

Word Count: 130

Glossary Links
strength
crave

  Tell about a BMX bike. Write two or three words.

❶ The Skywalkers' Challenge

Constructing big **bridges** and skyscrapers takes lots of skill. It is a big **challenge** to stand hundreds of feet up on a **ledge,** suspended over a vast space. This is a difficult but critical job.

Some of the most talented builders in the U.S. and Canada were brave Mohawk Indian men. They risked their lives to construct big buildings and **bridges.**

In 1886, Mohawk men helped construct a frame on a big **bridge** in Canada.

Then, some went on to help construct the king-sized Empire State Building, as well as the magnificent Twin Towers in Manhattan.

People were amazed that the men could balance on such thin metal beams. They admired and respected their talent and skill. They gave them the name "skywalkers."

Glossary Links
constructing
skyscrapers

Word Count: 107

 Why might "skywalkers" be a good name for the Mohawk builders?

Email

❷ The Golden Gate Bridge

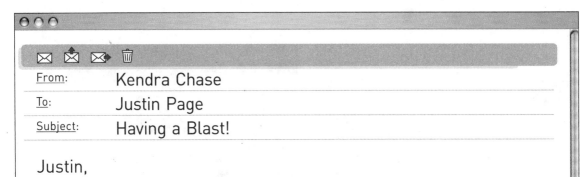

From: Kendra Chase

To: Justin Page

Subject: Having a Blast!

Justin,

I am having a fun time visiting San Francisco. :-) The Golden Gate **Bridge** is a **gem**! There's not much fog, just lots of sun. I spent **ages** shopping and got a lot of nice stuff. I am bringing you back a gift I got at the **bridge**. I am not telling you what it is!

Last night, I saw a **magic** act on **stage** with my mom and dad. A **strange** man in a cape locked himself in a **cage**. Then the **cage** was placed inside a big tank filled with water. Such suspense! I was on the **edge** of my seat. The man escaped OK. No problem! :-o

C U soon!

Kendra :-)

Word Count: 123

Glossary Links
suspense
on the edge of my seat

 Tell about one thing Kendra did in San Francisco.

1 A Commitment to Fitness

To the Editor,

I am writing to tell you that I liked your article on **fitness** last month.

Like you, I think that having a **fitness** plan is a must. I think that stretching is the best thing a person can do to get toned and fit.

Hitting the **pavement**, or gentle walking, has lots of benefits, too. And jogging can help a person get fit.

I tell my clients that **fitness** is not a **punishment**. It is a big **commitment**. It can give them a sense of **contentment** and can help fend off **illness.**

Getting a **fitness** plan is the best thing we can do to stay strong and in top shape.

Best,
Chuck Wong
Shape Up! Gym

Word Count: 119

Glossary Links
commitment
contentment

Do you agree with this writer about fitness? Tell why or why not.

❷ Run With Quickness

Can you run as fast as a rabbit? Well, these running tips can help take your run to the next level!

1. Begin with a nice, gentle jog.

2. Pick up your pace. You can run on grass, sand, and **pavement.**

3. Do not smack the **pavement** as you run. It can be a **punishment** on your legs.

4. Swing your arms forward and back, not side to side.

5. Tuck your chin in and keep your neck still. Avoid nodding. It can stress your spine.

6. Change your running pace from time to time. Sprint in quick, fast dashes. Then take it slow. Run up and down hills if you can. This will lift your **fitness** level!

Make a **commitment** to run often and get fit!

Word Count: 130

Glossary Links
sprint
dashes

Tell two things a person can do to run better.

❶ Telling a Good Joke

Did your last **joke** get a laugh? If not, do not give up **hope.** These tips can help make your **joke** a big success.

Glossary Links
punch line
chuckle

- Know a **joke** and tell it well.

- Pick **jokes** that your friends will like. Bad **jokes** will send them away fast!

- The punch line at the end of the **joke** will make a **joke** funny. Stop just before the punch line. This makes people pay **close** attention.

- Faces and hands can help tell a **joke,** too. Make faces or wave your hands**.** Use odd voices. This can make a **joke** funnier.

And if your **joke** is still a dud, just go with it. Say, "Well, I **suppose** I will give up my plan to be a comic!" That might get a chuckle!

Word Count: 126

 Who is your favorite comic performer? Tell why.

Humor

❷ The Joke's on You!

I asked Mom what a pest is. She stated that a pest is an annoying person, animal, or thing. Mom gave an example and said rats and mice are pests because they nibble on things, like **ropes** and wires.

I asked Dad what pests bug him. Dad said **moles** bug him because they dig **holes** and make **molehills** out back. Dad also dislikes red fire ants that bite.

I then made the mistake of asking Cole, my big brother, if he could name some pests besides rats, mice, and **moles.**

Cole **joked,** "That's simple! You're the biggest pest there is!"

Word Count: 100

Glossary Links
nibble
molehills

 Name one thing that bugs you. It can be a person, animal, or thing.

❶ A Huge (and Fun) Job

Dogs are **cute** and **amusing.** Lots of kids like dogs. But having a dog is a **huge** job. It takes a lot of time. You must fill a dog's dish with fresh kibble. You must walk a dog even when it is not nice outside, and you cannot make **excuses!**

- Dogs will nibble on lots of things, such as socks. So place socks and other things where a dog cannot get at them.

Glossary Links
kibble
instill

- Get a crate or a gate. **Use** it to make your dog safe when you are not at home.

- If your dog is bad, tell it fast. Punishing a dog after the fact can just **confuse** the dog.

Treat your dog well. This will instill its trust in you. It will also help you have lots of nice times with your pet.

Word Count: 135

 What does a dog need? Write two things.

❷ A Tribute to Amelia Bloomer

Back in the early 1800s, Amelia Bloomer was not thrilled with the customs of her time. She wished that getting dressed was not such a constant punishment. She **disputed** the fact that women had to dress in hot, thick clothing and stiff corsets. She wished that long dresses did not make taking big steps so difficult. And she felt that long dresses did not help much. In fact, she **fumed** each time she had to get dressed in a long dress.

Then in the 1850s, Amelia spotted a friend in big cotton pants. Amelia liked pants a lot. Pants like this could make life simple! Amelia chose to dress in these pants and recommended that others dress in them as well. It did not take long until things changed. The pants, named "bloomers," became a hot trend!

Glossary Links
corset
tribute

But the press was not **amused** at this trend. The press made so much fun of the pants that lots of women stopped dressing in them. Even Amelia stopped dressing in the bloomers.

But Amelia's last name lives on as a **tribute** to this past fashion craze.

Word Count: 170

 What is your favorite fashion trend?

❶ Ruthless Reptile!

A crocodile is a **reptile.** A **reptile** is a cold-blooded animal that has scales. A **reptile's** body temperature is the same as the temperature of its habitat.

A crocodile, or croc, lives in habitats such as rivers, lakes, or wetlands. A croc likes to dine on fish and mammals. A croc can be huge. It can get as big as 20 feet long. It can weigh as much as 2,000 pounds! But its long, thin shape helps it swim fast.

Despite its huge size, a croc is a fast and skilled hunter. A croc sits and waits for an unsuspecting animal to get close. If an animal makes the **mistake** of getting too close to a croc, the croc will grab it with its very strong jaws. If the animal cannot **escape,** it will be dragged under water. When this happens, it's **lunchtime!**

Word Count: 144

Glossary Links
temperature
unsuspecting

 Write two facts about crocodiles.

Letter

❷ Contribute Now!

Bandmates,

Our trip to L.A. is getting close, and we need to raise cash fast! I **compute** that we still need 500 bucks.

I think each section can **contribute**. The **trombones** are selling **lemonade** at home games. They will make it nice and fresh, and sell it for 3 bucks a cup. The drums are doing a bike wash. They think they can scrub about 50 bikes and make about 100 bucks fast.

Invite your mom and dad to our Big Band Dance party. Tickets will cost just 5 bucks. And bring **classmates** to our big bake sale. We will be selling snacks and **lemonade**.

This is the plan. Let's make some cash!

Bridget

Word Count: 114

Glossary Links
compute
contribute

Imagine you need to raise some cash.
What could you do?

❶ Letters to *The Tribune*

To the Editor,

    I **oppose** the plan to block Fifth Street with planters and shrubs. It will make traffic jams on Sixth and Seventh.

    This plan will help the residents on Fifth. But the rest of us will pay the **price.** Help stop this **mistake!**

Sixth St. Resident

To the Editor,

    Those who **oppose** the Fifth Street plan are **mistaken.** Their facts are **inflated**. I also **dispute** their **statements** about traffic.

    My **advice** is that people check the facts. See my blog **online**!

Fifth St. Resident

Word Count: 86

Glossary Links
shrubs
pay the price

 What is an issue that concerns you? Tell about it.

❷ A Bug to Admire

A male giant Water Bug makes an excellent dad. The Water Bug mom lays 150 eggs. Then she sticks them on the male's back. His job is to keep the eggs safe until they hatch. And he cannot make a **mistake!**

The male's job is to pet his eggs so the eggs will not get a bad fungus. And he has to bob up and down so the bugs **inside** the eggs will get air. He has to watch so that predators do not attack his eggs.

Glossary Links
fungus
predators

If the male bug does his job well, the **entire** batch will hatch. He will kick the empty eggshells off his back. Next, he will wait for his mate to stick the next big batch of eggs on his back. Then the dad must do his job again.

Word Count: 135

 Tell one thing a male Water Bug does.

Advice

1 Lunch Nonsense

Dear Meg,

I invited Brit and Alex to lunch. And let's just say, it did not go well. My plan was to make grilled chicken. I did not **defrost** the chicken in time. Lunch was late. This stressed me out. Then I burned the chicken AND Mom's **nonstick** grill pan!

Mom used a bunch of chicken bits that were not burned. Mom made us chicken sandwiches. Then my sister, Jan, chatted **nonstop** as we ate lunch. Plus, Jan ate all the ripe plums. She left just the **unripe** plums for us.

I cannot invite Brit and Alex to lunch again! This lunch was a mess!

Deflated

Dear **Deflated,**

Nonsense! Mistakes can happen, and I bet nobody had a bad time! If Brit and Alex are good friends, they will be back.

Meg

Word Count: 132

Glossary Links
stressed me out
ripe

 What is Deflated's problem?

② A Nonstop Process

Little organisms live in the soil. They help plants and animals rot and **decompose.** These **decomposed** plants and animals make soil rich. That helps plants to grow. This process is **nonstop.** It is a fact of life.

At the same time, trash is filling up landfills. A useful method of handling trash is *composting*. That is when a person collects grass clippings, pine cones, and kitchen scraps such as vegetables, rice, and eggshells. They put this stuff in a bin and let it rot.

Glossary Links
organisms
process

Animal products, such as chicken and fish scraps, should not go in the bins. That is because they can attract **uninvited** pests, such as ants and rats.

As trash sits and rots, it will **decompose.** Then it can be used in planting fresh gardens. This is a fine way to help the planet and make use of the little things we toss in the trash.

Word Count: 145

Would you like to compost? Why or why not?

❶ Gliding in Thin Air

Imagine this! You stand underneath a huge kite that has a big metal frame. The frame has a metal bar. Grasping the bar, you jog with a rapid pace down a gentle slope. As you run, the brisk wind lifts the kite up. And you rise up with it as well! Up, up, up!

You stretch your legs until your body is prone, or flat. You shift the frame from side to side, **changing** the kite's direction. It is such a rush to glide like a jet plane.

Not bad? Well, that is hang **gliding!** Hang **gliding** is fun and **exciting!**

Word Count: 101

Glossary Links
imagine
prone

 How do you change directions in a hang glider?

Email

➋ Trading Places

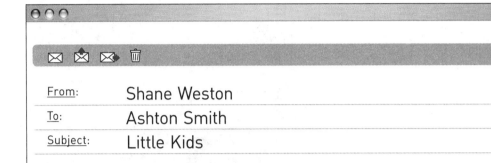

From: Shane Weston
To: Ashton Smith
Subject: Little Kids

Ashton,

What is the latest on your cousins? Isn't your mom expecting you to amuse the little kids this week? Man, that's **frustrating.** I'm glad I'm not you!

Shane

From: Ashton Smith
To: Shane Weston
RE: Little Kids

Shane,
I am in luck! My uncle invited us to Lake Chaplin with him. He said he will take the kids **hiking, skating, biking,** and **wading.** I don't have to watch them much at all! I will spend time on fun stuff like fishing, **diving,** and hang **gliding!** Bet you'd like **trading** places with me!

Ashton

Word Count: 104

 Write a reply from Ashton to Shane.

Glossary Links
wading
hang gliding

Fiction

① Scrubbing Jake

I went **jogging** with my dog, Jake. Jake spotted a pond. I had no chance of **stopping** him. In went Jake in a flash!

Swimming is one thing Jake cannot resist. But, man, did that pond make him smell bad!

When I got home, my friend Brandon was at my place.

"Yikes, that dog smells bad!"

"No **kidding!**" I said. I asked him to help give Jake a bath.

Jake does not like baths one bit. Brandon discovered what it is like to give Jake a bath. Brandon and I spent ten minutes **dragging** Jake into the tub. **Getting** him to stay in the tub was harder still! But Brandon and I did not plan on **quitting.**

Glossary Links
in a flash
resist

At last, Jake decided he had no chance of **winning.** He let us finish the job. But Jake got back at us! That bath got Brandon and me just as wet as Jake!

Word Count: 150

 Why does Jake need a bath?

Fiction

2 Pinch Hitting

Stepping up to home plate, Justin felt like **quitting. Batting** was not his strength and the game depended on him.

His first hit was a strike. Who was he **kidding?** He could not get a big enough hit to bring in the players on base. Strike two!

Scanning the sidelines, Justin saw his mom and dad with big smiles on their faces. **Gripping** the bat, Justin was not **admitting** defeat. Swinging his bat at the next fast pitch, he felt a crack as it hit his bat. Up, up, up it went, passing over the back fence. A home run!

Jogging into home plate, Justin felt a rush of pride as his teammates slapped him on the back. Good job!

Word Count: 120

Glossary Links
sidelines
teammates

 How did Justin feel after making a home run?

Fiction

❶ Visited by Ms. Rush

Ellen Rush is running for president. She visited us in class. She spoke about things like taxes, jobs, and saving the environment.

Then, Ms. Rush **joked** that her life as a candidate is a little strange. She said it was a big adjustment to have guards at her side when she shops and jogs.

Ms. Rush **smiled** and **waved** at us as she left. I **liked** her because she spent time chatting with kids in our class.

I have not **voted** yet. But in just six months, I will be 18. I think I will cast a vote for Ms. Rush! I hope she wins. I think she will make a fantastic president.

Glossary Links
environment
candidate

Word Count: 113

 What might you ask a presidential candidate? Write two questions.

Fable

❷ Puzzled by Nature?

A traveling man stopped and **dozed** under a big nut tree. When he woke up, he saw a huge pumpkin growing on a thin vine.

"Nature is not wise," the man said to himself. "If I had made the world, this big, strong tree would grow huge pumpkins, and that thin vine would grow nuts. It makes little sense as it is."

Just then, a little nut fell and hit him smack on top of his head!

Puzzled, he **gazed** up at the thick branches. Then, he **smiled** and **chuckled.**

He said, "It is I who am unwise! If it had been a big pumpkin that had landed on my head, it would have killed me!"

Word Count: 116

Glossary Links
dozed
unwise

What is the moral, or message, of this story?

Fiction

❶ A Badly Planned Surprise

I was in the middle of making bran pancakes for Mom's birthday. Then, I heard Mom chatting with Dad.

Oh no! Mom was already up! This was supposed to be a big surprise!

I **grabbed** the pancake mix and **crammed** it on a shelf in the fridge.

Then, in a huge panic, I tossed mixing bowls, eggs, bran, and milk inside the wastebasket!

Glossary Links
supposed
surprise

Just then, Mom **stepped** in the kitchen. She was already dressed. She **stopped** and said, "Yum, I smell pancakes. It's not Dad's birthday, is it?"

What? I must have mixed up the date! It looks like the surprise was on me!

Word Count: 104

 Have you ever been surprised? Tell about it.

Essay

❷ I Visited L.A.!

The Class Trip
By Nicole Simms

Last week our class visited Los Angeles. That is in California! We went to a lot of places. We did some really fun stuff.

Los Angeles Area

SANTA MONICA
VENICE BEACH
Marina del Rey
EL SEGUNDO
MANHATTAN BEACH
Pacific Ocean
ERMOSA BEACH
REDONDO BEACH
PALOS VERDES ESTATES
ROLLING HILLS
LONG BEACH
Pt. Vicente Park
Los Angeles Harbor
CABRILLO BEACH

I think Venice Beach is the best thing in L.A.! It's got lots and lots of sun, sand, and shops. People hang out on the boardwalk. On the boardwalk, people make and sell lots of things. I **shopped** and **shopped** until I **dropped.**

Musicians sang as they **drummed** and **strummed** instruments. I saw a man who **hopped** on his left leg, **sipped** a glass of milk, and juggled six big, fat, red apples at the same time. Incredible!

On the last day, I went bodysurfing. I got **flipped** by a huge wave. But I was fine. I think swimming in the ocean was the best thing yet.

This was a fantastic class trip!

Word Count: 143

Tell one thing Nicole likes about L.A.

Glossary Links
boardwalk
juggled

❶ Spy Nancy Wake

In films, James Bond is a well-known British **spy.** But Nancy Wake was a brave French **spy** in real life.

In World War II, Nancy smuggled messages across enemy lines. One time, Nancy rode a bike more than 100 miles carrying radio codes.

The Germans suspected that Nancy was a **spy.** Yet, they could not catch her. They gave Nancy a code name, White Mouse.

Nancy's life was constantly at risk. She attempted to leave France lots of times. At last, Nancy made it on her sixth **try.** Then, she went to London and got a job as a British **spy.**

Nancy says it was a big help being a woman at that time. This made it simple to slip past enemy lines. People did not suspect that Nancy was a **spy.**

Nancy Wake was a brave **spy.** She was admired and got lots of medals for risking her life and helping the French in difficult times.

Word Count: 158

Glossary Links
smuggled
radio codes

What was Nancy's code name?

Profile

❷ This Guy Can Fly!

A man named Miles Hilton-Barber cannot see. But Miles will not let that stop him from **trying** lots of thrilling things.

Miles has **skydived** 40 times. He has traveled from city to city across the globe. Miles has scaled the tallest mountains on the planet. Miles has raced for hundreds of miles in **dry,** hot deserts and freezing ice.

Miles will not even **shy** away from **flying**. Miles can **fly** a microlight plane. He uses a computer to help him **fly** it. Miles is the first blind man to **try flying** such a plane.

Glossary Links
deserts
microlight plane

Miles is on a quest to get as much from life as possible. He will not let anything stop him. On his Web site, Miles tells us, "The only limits in our lives are those we accept ourselves."

Word Count: 133

What might Miles Hilton-Barber say if you said you couldn't do something?

❶ Is Cricket Trendy?

Would you check out a cricket match in your town or **city?** That's cricket the game, not the bug!

A long time ago in the U.S., lots of fans liked the game cricket. Fans went to cricket matches and played in them as well. Fans included Benjamin Franklin. He came back from England in 1744 with a printed **copy** of cricket's rules.

But, as time went on, cricket lost its fans to baseball. Baseball is not as **tricky** as cricket. It is a fast game. It uses less equipment than cricket as well. By 1870, 2,000 baseball clubs had sprung up. Cricket was vanishing in the U.S.!

But cricket is back. And it is **trendy!** Immigrants from places like Pakistan and the Caribbean are helping to bring back the game. For cricket fans, this is **lucky.** They are **happy** that the game has made such a big comeback.

Glossary Links
immigrants
comeback

Now, almost 30,000 people in the U.S. play cricket. And that number is rising. Look out, baseball!

Word Count: 165

 What is your favorite sport? Tell about it.

Fiction

② A Risky Trip

Remy was **angry.** "Come on, Alix! Let's go!"

"Just a second," Alix said. "Let me finish packing my backpack. Did you pack yours?"

"Do not be **silly!** I don't need a backpack!" Remy insisted.

Remy and Alix set off on their hike. The path was steep and **rocky.** After a bit, Remy snapped, "I am so **hungry,** I am **dizzy.**"

"Let's take a rest," Alix suggested. "I packed **plenty** of snacks."

"It must be **ninety** degrees in the shade," Remy grumbled.

Alix gave Remy a sun hat from her backpack.

> **Glossary Links**
> steep
> compass

Then Remy said, "I think we are lost!"

"It's OK, Remy. I packed a compass and a map." Alix added, "And in case it gets **chilly,** I packed jackets, matches for a fire, and a whistle in case we get lost. I have lots of **safety** equipment."

"I am sorry, Alix," Remy admitted. "Next time I will take time to pack well before I go on a long hike."

Word Count: 159

 Tell about a time you were wrong. What happened?

❶ A Clever Gym Plan

Syd brags about his trips to the **gym.**

Syd tells Lynn, "I do not spend a lot of time in the **gym.** I made up a **system** to get in and out of the **gym** quick."

"Tell me about this **system**," Lynn says. "I spend too much time at the **gym.**"

"Well, I get to the **gym**," Syd says. "Then I listen to a nice classical song in my headphones."

"I am amazed, Syd! That music is quite slow!"

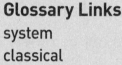

Glossary Links
system
classical

"It can be, but it is part of my '**gym system**.' But next is the best part. I take a nice long rest in the **gym's** hot tub."

Lynn smiles. "Just a sec, Syd. A rest? You must be joking! How do you get in shape?"

Syd adds with a smile, "Well, I sprint to the **gym.** I take a long rest while I am at the **gym.** Then I run home."

"That is a crazy **system!**" Lynn says with a grin. "I have to try it!"

Word Count: 166

 Do you have an exercise plan? Tell about it.

Email

❷ Cyndy's Email

From: Cyndy Hamilton

To: Efren Chavez

Subject: What's Up?

Efren,

Hey, what's up? Did you win the big game? I hope you made at least ten baskets! :-) You said you planned to run laps if you did not win. If you ask me, that seems a bit silly! No offense! :-)

I just got back from band. We played a song that ends with lots of **cymbals** crashing. A bunch of kids kept banging their **cymbals** and would not stop. Mr. Tilly got mad at the entire class.

I have **gymnastics** tomorrow. It's in the **gym**. At the last **gymnastics** class, I fell flat on my face. Yikes! I just felt like quitting after that. I am still a little bit stiff. But Miss Drake said that if I take extra time to stretch, I should be fine.

Write back!

Cyndy

Word Count: 140

Glossary Links
offense
cymbals

 Write two words that describe Cyndy.

Social Studies Nonfiction

1 Lucky to Be Alive!

In 1972, a plane crashed in the Andes Mountains. A rugby team was traveling on this plane. The plane slid **rapidly** on a **frosty** slope. **Sadly,** it crashed and got stuck in ice.

The crash had smashed the plane's radio. The plane had little food. Outside, the wind felt quite **chilly.** In fact, it felt like ice!

The crash survivors acted **quickly.** They melted ice and made fresh drinking water. They made blankets and flimsy snowshoes with things taken from the plane.

At last, the frost melted and a band of men went on a hike. It was **risky,** but they had to get help. The men were **lucky.** They stumbled upon a man who went and got help. At last, planes came **quickly** to take them **safely** home. Seventy-two days had passed since the plane crash. They were **lucky** to be alive!

Word Count: 144

^^ Andes Mountains

Glossary Links
survivors
snowshoes

Write two questions you might ask a crash survivor.

Science Nonfiction

❷ Slimy Slugs

What travels on one foot, spends the winter napping, and can bite? A slug!

If you think a slug is icky, think again. A slug has amazing hidden talents. For one thing, it looks like it is sliding on its belly. But it is really gliding on a single **sticky, slimy** foot.

A slug has four long, thin tentacles. This helps it smell, see, and feel along its path as it travels.

As fall ends, a slug digs a hole in mud. It must stay wet or it will die. It slides inside its tunnel and dozes **snugly** until spring. Then, it wakes up and **quickly** hunts for plants to snack on with its many teeth.

Glossary Links
tentacles
tunnel

You might think a slug is just an ugly bug. But it is not. In fact, slugs are very interesting!

Word Count: 136

 Write one fact about slugs.

1 Amazing Mummies

When humans die, their skin and organs decompose. A lot of the time, just the skeleton is left. But, sometimes, **bodies** can dry up and become **mummies.** Things like sand, dry wind, and ice have **dried** out **bodies** and kept them from decomposing.

The Iceman is a mummy from over 5,300 years ago. He was spotted in the Italian Alps. This man probably hid in a space in the rocks to escape his **enemies.** Then he got stuck in a bad snowstorm. He ended up getting frozen. But his body did not decompose. It became a mummy. **Luckily** for us, scientists can study the Iceman's **dried** body. It tells them a lot about his life and his habits.

Glossary Links
organs
decompose

Another mummy is Tollund Man. He was **spied** in a wetland in Denmark. Tollund Man is over 2,000 years old. The study of his body has uncovered lots of facts about his life.

Thanks to **mummies** like the Iceman and Tollund Man, scientists can study what life was like in the past.

Word Count: 170

 Who is the Iceman? Write one or two sentences.

Profile

② Nadia Flies!

In films, it seems like the impossible is possible. Characters in films fly through the **skies,** dive from planes, jump from speeding vans, and do lots of amazing things. And they land safely without as much as a scratch on them!

It is true that films can be thrilling. And a lot of the time, it takes an amazingly brave person to make a film exciting. "Fearless Nadia" was an actress like that. In fact, she was celebrated for her stunts.

Nadia's true name was Mary Ann Evans. In India, Evans acted in more than fifty classic films in the 1930s, 1940s, and 1950s.

Glossary Links
stunts
special effects

Because Evans came from Australia, her face and habits struck her fans as exotic. And at that time, it was not common for women to act in public or in films. But Evans did not let this stop her. In fact, Evans **tried** to excite fans with astonishing stunts as she **supplied** timeless film moments. And it was a gamble. Evans did not use straps, nets, **dummies,** or special effects in the stunts. But **luckily,** Evans did not get badly hurt. In fact, Evans lived to be 88!

Word Count: 192

 When did Fearless Nadia act in films?

❶ Whale Spotting

You stand on the deck of a ship. You are gazing at the sea. Suddenly, you spot a splash. In a flash, a huge **whale** is poking out of the water. A **whale** has spotted you. And you have just spotted a **whale**—probably a humpback **whale!**

A **whale** spends its entire life in water. But **whales** are mammals. And, like all mammals, **whales** have lungs. A **whale** must come up and take in oxygen from time to time. **When** this happens, you might spot it behaving in some fascinating ways.

For example, a humpback **whale** likes to *spyhop*. That is **when** a **whale** pops up and takes a quick look around. **When** a **whale** jumps up, it is *breaching*. If it lies still and rests, it is *logging*. **When** it **whips** up its tail and slaps it back down with a splash, it is *lobtailing*.

Glossary Links
mammals
migrate

Whales migrate from place to place. **Whales** travel north in the spring to feed. And they swim south in the fall to mate. **Whales** are amazing animals. It is thrilling to spot a **whale** as it makes its trip!

Word Count: 185

 Why do whales come up from the water?

Profile

❷ Alexandra Courtis Is a Whiz

At age 17, Alexandra Courtis did not drive. She did not spend much time shopping. She did not spend a lot of time sitting at home gazing at the TV.

Alexandra did spend much of her time in a lab. **While** in the lab, she invented a process that spots cancer cells. This process is a big step in the long battle to diminish the risks of getting cancer.

As a little kid, Alexandra was a **whiz.** She did things that were uncommon. At age 2, she composed sentences. At age 5, she could make sense of long novels.

Glossary Links
process
cancer

Still, she is like a lot of kids her age. She likes traveling. She likes helping the public and the planet. She likes dancing. And she likes tennis a lot.

Her commitment to science has not stopped her from trying to have a normal life.

Word Count: 144

 What are three things Alexandra likes to do? Tell two or three things you like to do.

❶ Elephants

The African **elephant** is the biggest land mammal on the planet. In fact, an adult African **elephant** can weigh as much as seven tons. An African **elephant's** mammoth size affects how it lives.

For example, because an African **elephant** is so big, it must eat a lot. In fact, an adult African **elephant** takes in up to 400 pounds of food a day. This helps it get the energy it needs. It must drink plenty of liquid as well. An African **elephant** uses its trunk to suck up as much as 30–50 gallons of liquid a day.

An African **elephant's** size affects where it travels to get food. Because an African **elephant** is so big, it uses a lot of energy to travel up slopes. Scientists estimate that an African **elephant** uses 25 times more energy to travel up a slope than to travel on flat land. So an African **elephant** tends to stick to flat land as it hunts. As a result, the **elephants** dine on grass and shrubs. These plants are common on flat lands.

> **Glossary Links**
> energy
> liquid

Studying how an African **elephant** lives is important. In fact, studying the **elephant** and tracking its travels can help African **elephants** survive. Scientists use these facts to help protect and save African **elephants'** habitats.

Word Count: 212

 Write two facts about African elephants.

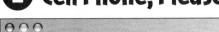

Email

❷ Cell Phone, Please!

From: Phil Rice

To: Frank Rice

Subject: Can I Get A Cell **Phone?**

Dad, can I get a cell **phone?**

From: Frank Rice
To: Phil Rice
RE: Can I Get A Cell **Phone?**
No, you cannot get a cell **phone.** They cost a lot. Besides, cell **phones** are just a fad.

From: Phil Rice
To: Frank Rice
RE: RE: Can I Get A Cell **Phone?**
Cell **phones** have lots of fantastic uses. I can use it to take photos of you and Mom! I can text **phrases** to you.

From: Frank Rice
To: Phil Rice
RE: RE: RE: Can I Get A Cell **Phone?**
Still no. Your mom and I hate having photos taken. Besides, we do not text.

From: Phil Rice
To: Frank Rice
RE: RE: RE: RE: Can I Get A Cell **Phone?**
Dad, if I had a cell **phone,** I could phone you if I am lost or will be late getting home. If I get in a jam, I could **phone** 911. What do you think?

From: Frank Rice
To: Phil Rice
RE: RE: RE: RE: RE: Can I Get A Cell **Phone?**
You are funny—and a **phony!** But, I will think about it. A cell **phone** may not be a bad thing. Let's chat at home;-)

Word Count: 203

At what age should kids get a cell phone? Tell why.

Glossary Links
fad
in a jam

Silent Consonants

❶ What's Wrong?

Word Count: 56

Glossary Links
off-key
adjusting

 Do you know a good joke? Tell it.

❷ Finding a Shipwreck

People like things **written** about **shipwrecks** and sunken treasures. After all, a ship that has sunk is like a huge time capsule. It can tell us a lot about the past.

Shipwrecks used to be much more common in the past. But ships still sink today. Strong winds, thick fog, raging fires, and other things can make a ship sink.

Sometimes a ship will drift in the **wrong** direction. Then, it can crash or **knock** against a huge rock, ice cap, or other ship. This can make a ship sink as well.

Divers can go inside some **shipwrecks** to study them. They may locate gems and historical objects. But if a **wreck** is a military ship, they cannot take its contents. That stuff must stay with the **wreck.**

Word Count: 129

Glossary Links
treasures
gems

What might a diver find on a shipwreck?
List three or four things.

Comic

1 A Cable Crisis

We will take it.

Pass the **bacon**.

This was the place! It **even** had a bedroom just for me. And it had a nice den to **relax** in. Plus, it was **vacant** so we could move right in. Yes!

The first thing we did was set up a **table.** Mom and Dad made a big plate of sandwiches.

We spent lots of time unpacking boxes. Then, we plopped down in the den just to **relax,** but...oh no! No **cable!**

Luckily, the **cable** man came quickly and fixed the problem. That was a close call!

Things are great in my house and life! Mom and Dad are happy, too. I like this place!

Word Count: 114

Why was the boy surprised?

Glossary Links
vacant
plopped

❷ The Dependable Truck

Tow trucks have many jobs. If a **vehicle** gets in a wreck and cannot move, a tow truck can take it to a safe, **vacant** spot. Then, it can get fixed. If a **vehicle** is stuck or spinning its tires on ice or in mud, a tow truck can quickly help get it out.

Tow trucks **frequently** pick up **vehicles** that sit in spots that are not **legal.** Drivers can get their **vehicles** back, but the fines can cost them a lot.

Glossary Links
wreck
fines

Tow trucks move **vehicles** in lots of ways. **Vehicles** can ride on a level **table** on a flatbed truck. Other trucks drag **vehicles** with a metal **cable.**

Spotting a tow truck can be a reason to get happy or mad. It just **depends** on whether it is there to help you or take your **vehicle** away!

Word Count: 138

 Tell what a tow truck does.

1 A Bonobo Named Kanzi

Bonobos are a kind of chimp. They live in the **Congo** in Africa. **Bonobos** are closely related to **humans.** And they are quite intelligent.

Kanzi is a **bonobo.** He is in a **program** in the **United** States that investigates **bonobos.** He lives with seven other **bonobos** in a **unit** that has 18 rooms. By pressing a button, he can **open** doors in the **unit.** He can get snacks from a vending machine. He can use a **microwave** in the kitchen. And he can **even** watch DVDs.

Glossary Links
vending machine
vocabulary

Kanzi has a huge vocabulary. He knows the meaning of 3,000 words in English. He can identify 348 lexigrams. A *lexigram* is a symbol that stands for the name of a thing.

Kanzi's keeper tells how one time he identified lexigrams for *marshmallows* and *fire*. She gave him sticks, matches, and marshmallows. Kanzi then lit a fire and toasted marshmallows on a stick!

Word Count: 150

 Tell three or four things that Kanzi can do.

❷ Secrets of America's Big Cat

Pumas are widely **distributed** across the Americas, from the **Yukon** in Canada to South America. These big cats live in many different habitats, such as dry, rocky deserts, as well as **humid** places.

A puma will track animals such as mice, rabbits, livestock, and elk.

While they will attack **humans,** such attacks are not common. **Humans** are simply not on this big cat's **menu!**

Instead, they can be shy and seldom seen. But it is wise to make noise while hiking. Bring a thick stick and do not hike alone.

Most likely the **moment** will never happen when you must confront this cat. But if you do come face-to-face with it, do not run. Stand up, wave your hands, make noises, and toss things at it. That will be the best **defense** against this cat!

Word Count: 137

Glossary Links
confront
defense

Imagine you are face-to-face with a puma.
Tell what happens.

❶ An Amazing Animal

Want to spot an **animal** with a striking but strange face? Take a look at a star-nosed mole.

This **animal** has an **amazing** nose. Its nose has 22 pink, fleshy **tentacles.** Otherwise, this mole looks a lot like a rat. It has thick, brownish fur. And its tail is long and scaly. The mole's **habitat** is in wetlands and **along** the banks of ponds and lakes.

The mole uses the pink, fleshy **tentacles** on its nose to **identify** food. It can smell worms, grubs, tiny shrimp, and insects this way. The **tentacles** have about 100,000 tiny nerves. They help the mole get its food quickly. It takes just a split second for a star-nosed mole to **identify** and gulp down a yummy snack!

Glossary Links
striking
nerves

Word Count: 126

 What is different about the nose of this mole?

❷ A Complicated Insect

Do you spend much time thinking about ants? Most people do not. It is common to think that an ant is just a pest. And it is common to think that, because an ant is tiny, it must be a simple insect. But this is not true! In fact, when we study an ant up close, we can see that an ant is a **magnificent** and **complicated** insect.

More than 12,000 kinds of ants exist today. And ants inhabit most places on the globe. But we do not see ants that much. That is because an ant's **habitat** is commonly underground. Ants construct big **colonies** that can have more than a million ants. And an ant **colony** is **divided** into a complex system of tunnels and rooms. Some rooms hold food. Some are **selected** to hold young ants until they become **adults. Colonies** can be quite complex. It is **amazing** ants do not get lost in them!

Glossary Links
inhabit
system

At times, people have spent time thinking about ants. In fact, ants have been **celebrated.** For example, in fables, ants can **represent** teamwork and success. While a fable is fiction, those traits really **define** ants.

Yes, ants are successful insects. In fact, if we add up all the organisms on our planet that dwell on land, 15% would be ants!

Word Count: 181

 Write two facts about ants.

❶ The Six Hills Shopping Complex

Have You Visited Six Hills Shopping Complex Yet? Well, Get On With It! Why Not?

- Take in a film at our brand new cinema **complex. Confess** it. You like new films. Films are fun!

- Shop until you drop! Six Hills has ten new **connected** shops where you can shop with **confidence!** Get dresses, slacks, hats, and jackets. Shop for games, sunglasses, TVs, **contact** lenses, and DVDs. You name it, Six Hills has it!

- **Connect** with friends and family. Dine in any of six fine dining establishments **committed** to your satisfaction. Or grab a quick bite and a drink at the Snack Stop. It has snacks from every **continent!**

- Six Hills shopping complex **combines** shopping, dining, and fun. You will be glad that you came!

Word Count: 125

Do you like to shop? Tell why or why not.

Glossary Links
complex
confidence

❷ Committed to Change

Ann,

I **confess.** I am filled with envy. My best friend Constance's room looks like it belongs to a teen. Mine looks like a little kid's.

I **commented** to my mom that my room does not reflect ME! She said that she will help me fix it up, but we cannot spend much.

I am totally **committed** to making it nice. Can you help us?

Conflicted

Conflicted,

Contemplate these quick fixes. They can change your space from drab to fab!

- Paint does not cost much, but it can make a big impact. **Combine** colors that will give your room some zing!

- **Construct** simple shelves with flat planks and bricks.

- Get a cozy bed cover with a fabric you like.

- It's simple to make drapes. Get a cloth that you like. Then just stitch a flap across the top.

- Finish your fun and funky look by adding little extras! Try hanging up music posters and photos that tell who you are!

Best of luck!
Ann

Word Count: 165

Glossary Links
envy
contemplate

Tell one thing you would change in your room.

❶ Training Rocky

Training a dog can be fun. But when you **train** a dog, the dog **trains** you as well. I discovered this when I **trained** my dog, Rocky.

I **trained** Rocky to sit. I held a little snack by his nose. Rocky made it **plain** that he was hungry. I lifted the dog snack over his head and then back by his **tail.**

I commanded Rocky to sit. I said, "Rocky, sit."

He sat, gazing constantly at the prize. The instant Rocky sat, I **exclaimed**, "Good dog!" I handed him the prize. He gobbled it in an instant, wagging his **tail.**

Now, every time Rocky sees me, he sits. Then, I give him a snack. Sometimes I think, "Hmmm, did I **train** Rocky, or did he **train** me?" Sometimes it is not so clear.

Word Count: 133

Glossary Links
commanded
gobbled

Why does the narrator think a dog can train its owner?

❷ A Painted History

Nails with crazy **nail** polish and fancy **details** on them are not a recent trend. In fact, humans have **painted** their **nails** for quite a long time.

Ladies in China began **painting** their **nails** about 5,000 years ago. Back then, things like wax, egg whites, vegetables, and mashed petals were mixed to make **nail** polishes. These pink and red tints **stained** the **nails.**

People of lower status who worked with their hands did not polish their **nails.** It just was not practical. And in some places, it was not even allowed!

Glossary Links
tints
status

In ancient Egypt, only rich gentlemen and ladies, kings and queens, and men going to battle **painted** their **nails.** Finely trimmed and **painted nails** demonstrated status. Red **stains** were used just by royalty. And polishing your **nails** in the same shade as the queen could get you **jail** time, or even worse!

Word Count: 144

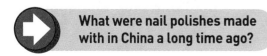
What were nail polishes made with in China a long time ago?

1 A Snow Day in Dubai

Dear Pen Pal,

My home is in Dubai. It is a city in the Middle East. **Days** here can be hot and dry. In fact, it is the last place on earth you might think to **play** in the snow. But inside a big shopping complex here, there are huge ski slopes with lots of artificial snow and ice.

When I visit the complex, the **midday** sun sizzles. Then, a frigid wind hits my face. I rent a jacket and mittens. Then, I stop to admire the white-tipped pine branches. I must quickly duck as some **stray** snowballs whiz past my face.

Next, I ride a lift up the chilly white slopes. At the top of the lift, I spot the biggest slope yet. (Thanks, but I think I'll pass!) But the bobsleds look like fun. I **may** just take a bobsled ride!

Even though Dubai is hot and sunny, this has got to be the best snow **day** yet!

Write back soon!

Your Pen Pal,
Ahmed

Word Count: 168

What snow activity interests you most? Tell why.

Glossary Links
Middle East
artificial

2 Stay in Shape

Get in shape and **stay** in shape! It will take work, but it will **pay** off in fitness and fun.

Jogging is a nice **way** to get in shape. But be safe! Do not run on ice or on slick roads. Run in the **daytime,** and **stay away** from traffic.

It is best to change your fitness plan from time to time. That **way** you tone more of your body and can avoid getting in a rut.

These things can help you get in shape and **stay** in shape:

- lift weights
- **play** sports
- skip rope
- jog or run
- do sit-ups
- stretch

Glossary Links
traffic
in a rut

Do your best to **stay** active. Make a fitness plan. And make sure you **stay away** from junk food! If you stick to these simple tips, you will be on your **way** to feeling great and looking good!

Word Count: 140

 List one or two things a person can do to stay fit.

Advice

❶ Why Can't She Explain?

Jay,

My best friend's name is Caitlin. Last **Sunday,** she made it **plain** that she doesn't think I act like a true friend. I asked Caitlin to **explain,** but she left in a huff. I hate to **complain,** but I miss my best friend. Help!

Daisy

Daisy,

I must **say** one thing—a true friend will help in **rain** or shine. True friends are there when things are fine—and will **stay** when things are bad as well.

True friends also take the time to listen. Daisy, go back and chat with Caitlin. Tell Caitlin that you will take the time to listen, but she must **explain** the problem. **Explain** that you want to **maintain** this friendship. Then, **say** you will help in any **way** that you can.

Jay

Word Count: 129

Glossary Links
made it plain
in a huff

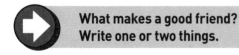

What makes a good friend?
Write one or two things.

Email

❷ The Laptop Complaint

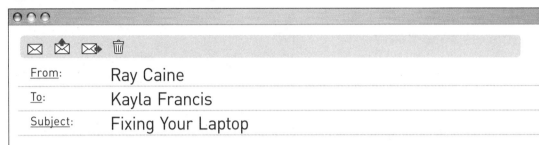

From: Ray Caine

To: Kayla Francis

Subject: Fixing Your Laptop

Hi, Kayla,

You asked me if you should **complain** to the manufacturer of your new laptop. I **say,** absolutely!

Based on what you described, that laptop has huge problems. When my laptop broke and I **complained,** they fixed it in less than ten **days.** I did not have to **pay** a thing.

This is what I did:

1. I phoned the company that made it.

2. I **explained** my problem in **detail.**

3. I asked them to either fix my laptop or send me a new one.

4. Then, I sent my laptop to them that **day.**

When I got it back, it ran just fine. So, go for it! Write back and tell me what happens, **okay?**

Ray

Word Count: 125

Glossary Links
manufacturer
company

 Have you ever had to send something back to the store or manufacturer? Tell about it.

Science Nonfiction

❶ What Makes Soap Float?

Did you ever think about what makes **soap float?**

Maybe you've noticed that some **soaps** will sink to the bottom of the tub. They can be slippery and difficult to find. But other **soaps** will just **float** up to the top.

In fact, even with the same brand of **soap,** you may find that some **soaps** sink and some **soaps float.**

What makes an object **float?** The ability to **float** depends on an object's density. *Density* is described as how heavy a thing is for its size. Take a tiny rock. It can be much denser than an object the same size, such as a **coat** button.

Glossary Links
density
liquid

If an object's density is less than a liquid's density, the object will **float** in that liquid. If it is not, then the object will sink in that liquid. It is as simple as that.

Lastly, some **soaps** contain lots of air bubbles. The bubbles help make **soap** light, and the bubbles help **soap** to **float!**

Word Count: 162

 Name two or three objects that can float.

❷ Callahan's Boat

In 1982, Steven Callahan made a homemade **boat** that he sailed to sea. After six days, the **boat** capsized in the middle of the Atlantic. A whale may have collided with his ship.

Steven had to abandon his **boat. Floating** alone on a life raft, Steven crafted a device called a *still*. The still made salt water into water he could drink. He made a simple spear to catch fish. But he did not have good luck, and was constantly hungry.

Each day, the sun's hot rays dried his skin. Sharks tried to attack him. Ships even passed by and missed him.

Glossary Links
capsized
spear

But Steven did not give up. After seventy-six difficult days and 1,800 miles **afloat,** Steven's luck changed. A fishing **boat** spotted him and rescued him!

Word Count: 129

 Tell about one problem Steven had at sea.

News Article

❶ A City Garden Grows

Class Grows a Garden

by Grace Chung

Students at Tate Middle School are studying what it takes to **grow** fresh vegetables in the middle of a city. Students constructed a greenhouse with many huge **windows.** "The **windows** let the plants get sun, even when it **snows**," says Tiffany Pinkins, a sixth-grade student.

Students filled boxes with rich topsoil. They planted lots of seeds. They set up a system of hoses. And they had to check that their plants got a decent water **flow**.

"Then we just waited," says student Antwon Hill. "But tiny plants popped up pretty quickly!" Teacher Mike Logan says students are graphing the plants' **growth.**

It will be late July when the vegetables are ripe and can be picked. Students will visit and tend the plants until then.

The students are thinking about ways that they can help younger kids. They hope to **show** them that it is fun and simple to **grow** a garden of their **own**.

Word Count: 162

Glossary Links
greenhouse
system

How did the class grow vegetables? List two or three things they did.

❷ Do You Know Stan Lee?

When you visit a comic shop, you will see **row** upon **row** of comics on the shelves. Most likely, you will see well-**known** comic titles like *Spider-Man*, *Blade*, *X-Men*, and *Fantastic Four*.

But did you **know** that the same man gave life to all of those famed comics? It's true! His name is Stan Lee.

Stan began writing comics as a kid. He tried to make comics that were unlike the rest. Stan insisted that his characters act like real people who just happen to be heroes. He wrote stories that people could connect with.

As a result, his widely admired tales have made lots of people **grow** to like comics. And he **showed** kids that reading can be fun, too.

Many films have been based on Stan's comics. And even after all this time, Stan's comics are still in top demand!

Word Count: 145

Glossary Links
characters
admired

 Do you like comics? Tell about your favorite ones.

❶ Who Owns the Roads?

Bobby Evans got sick of seeing trash **thrown** along the **roads** by his Texas home. He wondered what he could do. He didn't **own** the **roadways.**

One day in 1984, Evans **followed** a pickup truck. It had a **load** of rubbish that was **blowing** onto the **roadway.** As he **approached,** he had to dodge the trash. He knew he must act. So, in 1985, Evans began the "Adopt a Highway" program. He asked local clubs to tend **roads.** He asked them to pick up trash in specific places. The clubs began adopting the **roads.**

Today, every state has this program. Clubs and other groups pay to adopt a **roadway.** They pay the costs for picking up trash and maintaining the **road.**

> **Glossary Links**
> dodge
> adopt

Evans's program did not stop there. Places such as Canada and Japan began programs, too. Now, thanks to Evans, we can all **own** the **roads!**

Word Count: 150

 Tell about a street or lot that needs cleaning up.

② Danger on the Coast

A man named George Bennett settled on Oregon's **coast** in 1873. The settlement was named Bandon, after Bennett's home back in Ireland.

Bennett brought with him a plant named "gorse." This plant thrived in Bandon, growing fast and happily. Its **yellow** petals **coated** the **coastline** in gold.

In 1936, hot, dry winds blew a forest fire into Bandon. The thick gorse fed the blaze. Flames raged. The fire left hundreds of homes and shops in ashes. At least ten residents were killed.

Glossary Links
thrived
eliminate

The citizens of Bandon made it their **goal** to get rid of the gorse. It is close to impossible to eliminate the plant. But this did not stop the residents from trying. They chopped, yanked, cut, dug, sprayed, and **mowed** it. They sent in insects and animals to eat it. Yet, it still thrived.

Today, the Bandon **coastline** is still **coated** in gold. And those who **know** Bandon's past remain on edge, **knowing** that fire may come back at any time. But in the meantime, they are happy to gaze at the stunning **yellow** plant that lines their **coast.**

Word Count: 181

 Imagine you are a reporter. Write a paragraph about the fire in Bandon.

Prefixes *re-*, *pre-*

❶ An Idea to Rethink

I was sick of being broke. So when my uncle said he would hire me as a dog groomer, I decided this could be my big Get Rich Quick Plan.

"You're hired!" he said. "You can start by giving Scrappy a bath." He **prepaid** the $10 fee.

I planned to begin with Scrappy. Then I would get lots more jobs. I hoped to be the richest **preteen** in town.

Glossary Links
broke
shot

Scrappy is a little dog with a very strong will. He absolutely did not want a bath. He scratched me. He kicked me. And then he ran. I didn't know little dogs could run so fast! Finally I wrestled him into the tub. But he splashed constantly. I had to **refill** the tub twice.

I was soaked, and my day was shot. My uncle's ten bucks didn't seem like enough for what that dog had put me through! I have to **rethink** my plan. I'm hunting for a Get Rich Quick Plan B!

Word Count: 162

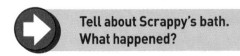

Tell about Scrappy's bath. What happened?

❷ The Rewriter's Life

I was so excited when I met novelist Tish Franklin at my local bookshop. I've always thought a writer's life must be quite thrilling.

I went up to her and asked, "How do you write your novels?"

Tish replied, "Well, I begin with **prewriting.** I must know everything about my characters' lives. So I research jobs, cities, and other cultures. Next, I **recheck** my facts. Then, I spend quite a while sitting at my desk writing my novel. But writing it is just the beginning."

Glossary Links
novelist
research

Tish explained, "I end up **rewriting** lots of times until I am happy with it."

"Are you kidding?" I asked, astonished.

"No, not at all," Tish said. **"Rewriting** is the most critical part of my job."

"That doesn't sound so thrilling!" I said.

Tish grinned. "Actually, when I have gotten my writing just the way I want it, it is the biggest thrill!"

Word Count: 150

 Name a thrilling job. Tell why you think so.

❶ Reaching His Goal

Life at Marcus Leach's high school was **bleak.** Kids got checked for guns **each** day. He did not like school. So Marcus spent his time playing games.

One day, the debate coach visited his class. She convinced him to take a debate class.

Debate **teams** collect evidence about a topic. They argue about topics with other debate **teams.** They must think quickly. They must know facts. They must develop a talent for public **speaking.** In a debate, the **team** with the best arguments wins.

Glossary Links
bleak
evidence

Marcus realized that he liked debating. And he began **reading** constantly.

Marcus became a champ at debate. He went up against the best **teams** in the U.S. He debated teams with rich kids who spent time at debate camps. These kids did not **dream** that he could **beat** them. But he did!

When Marcus **reached** the twelfth grade, debating paid off. A college invited him to attend. They asked him to debate with their **team.** In return, he could attend college at no cost.

Word Count: 168

 What do debate teams do?

❷ Beach Clean-Up Day

I was not happy when Dad made me help with **Beach Clean-**Up Day.

"We like the **beach,**" he told me. "So the **least** we can do is help **clean** it up."

"I've got other things to do today," I grumbled. Dad shrugged and kept picking up trash.

At the **beach, teams** of volunteers with sacks were hiking and picking up all kinds of stuff. I picked up one or two crumpled cans, a glass bottle, and a plastic bag. **Each** was coated with a thick, black slime. It was disgusting!

Glossary Links
volunteers
crumpled

Then, I spotted a shiny piece of **sea** glass. I tucked it in the pocket of my **jeans.** I picked up more trash until I came across a beautiful **seashell** and a glass fishing float. The fishing float looked like a big bubble with more bubbles inside it.

That's when it struck me! I was not just picking up trash. I was hunting for treasure!

Word Count: 156

What did the narrator find at the beach? Name two or three things.

1 The Lighthouse Keeper

George Taylor was a lighthouse keeper along the east coast in the 1850s. Taylor had a huge dog named Milo.

Milo helped in lots of ways. When **deep** fog came in, Milo barked at the approaching **fleets.** This let the ships know to avoid the big rocks close by. Taylor claimed that his dog's signal helped **keep** ships safe as much as his lighthouse did.

Men who fished close to the beach liked to play a game with Milo. They would slip a slab of codfish on a stick and then throw the stick out to sea. Then Milo would swim as much as a mile to get the stick! Clutching the stick in his **teeth,** Milo swam back to land. There, his family had fresh codfish to eat.

But Milo was best-known for saving children. In fact, a man named Edwin Landseer painted Milo with his son in a painting named, *Saved.* Milo was a trusted family pet who became well-known around the globe.

Glossary Links
lighthouse
fleets

Word Count: 169

 Tell about other jobs that animals do.

❷ Deep, Deep Quicksand

Have you **seen** a **creepy** TV show where a man steps into quicksand? His **feet** vanish. Then, his **knees** vanish as well. Soon, he is in so **deep** that the quicksand has sucked him in. In real life, quicksand is not like that.

Quicksand is just a mix of sand and water. It is found in inland spots near lakes and marshes and at beaches. Quicksand is not more than a few **feet deep.**

While quicksand can be strong, it cannot pull a human being under.

Glossary Links
vanish
thrashing

But if you happen to step into **deep** quicksand, what should you do? The main thing is to stay still and do not panic. Thrashing in quicksand will just make you sink in deeper.

So, relax. Swim slowly to the top. Then, lie back until you float to safety.

That is the secret to surviving quicksand!

Word Count: 142

 How might quicksand feel? Write three words.

❶ A Niece's Mistake

MISSING!

A blue police hat that belongs to **Chief** Patrick Lane. His **niece** "borrowed" it last week. She needed it for a costume party. Sadly, that **niece** lost it on her way home. She thinks she may have dropped it in a **field** off Black Rock Road.

Chief Lane needs his hat back! There is a $50 reward to the person who **retrieves** it and brings it back to the local precinct. No questions asked.

P.S. Uncle Patrick, I am so, so sorry! **Believe** me—next time I will ask before I take your hat!

Glossary Links
niece
precinct

Word Count: 96

Have you ever lost something important? Tell about it.

❷ The Chiefs and the Bobcats

Caleb ran onto the **field.** It was his first home game playing for the **Chiefs.**

Students and parents **shrieked** in the stands. They roared, "You can beat them, **Chiefs!**" and "Go get 'em, Bobcats!"

Then the ball was in play. Caleb blocked for the quarterback. He protected him from an approaching linebacker. Thanks to Caleb's skills, the quarterback had time to make a long pass.

Glossary Links
blocked
yielded

Within just five **brief** minutes, the **Chiefs** scored! Fans stomped, clapped, and chanted. They yelled, "Win, **Chiefs,** Win!"

The Bobcats were struck by how quickly they had **yielded** points. They asked for a time-out.

At that time, the **Chiefs'** coach instructed his team, "Keep on playing just like Caleb, and we will win this game!"

Caleb blushed. His face flashed red. He had never felt so much pride in his life!

Word Count: 136

 Tell about a time when you felt proud.

Science Nonfiction

❶ America's Bald Eagles

Three hundred years ago, bald **eagles** were quite common in the United States. Scientists estimate that in 1700, there were **between** 300,000 and 500,000 bald **eagles.** That number **decreased** significantly to just 20,000 **eagles** by 1950. And by 1960, there were fewer than 1,000 **eagles.**

This drastic **decrease** was mainly caused by humans. Following World War II, **fields** and crops were sprayed with a bug-killing liquid called DDT. DDT washed off plants and **leaked** into lakes and **streams.** Plants and little animals absorbed it. Fish ate the plants and animals. And then **eagles** ate the tainted fish. As a result, DDT made **eagles** lay eggs that had thin, **weak** shells. These eggs failed to hatch.

Glossary Links
absorbed
tainted

In 1972, DDT was widely banned in the U.S. And since then, bald **eagles** have made an amazing comeback. Today, more than 65,000 **eagles** live in the U.S.

Word Count: 149

 Tell why bald eagles are making a comeback.

Life Skills Nonfiction

❷ Sleepy Teens!

It may not shock you, but a **teen** dozing in class may not be getting enough **sleep!** A daily dose of at **least** nine hours of **sleep** is **ideal.** Yet only about 20% of **teens** get that much **sleep.**

Why can't **teens sleep?** A big **reason** is that lots of **teens** can't fall **asleep** until late at night. Yet, they still **need** to get up for class on time the next day. Family problems and stress can also affect **teens** and **keep** them up late at night.

Glossary Links
concentrate
schedule

Studies show that the risks for **sleep-**deprived **teens** are huge. These **teens** may be less active. They concentrate less, get lower grades, and **feel** depressed more than **teens** who get plenty of **sleep.**

If you have problems getting to **sleep** at night, try following these simple tips:

- do not drink coffee, tea, or cola after lunchtime.
- follow the same **sleep** schedule each day. Go to bed and get up at the same time on **weekdays** and **weekends.**
- spend less time online and watch less TV before bed.

Word Count: 177

What are some effects of not getting enough sleep?

❶ Insight Into a Dog's Mind

Dogs speak to us without words. They tell us what they are thinking and feeling by using signals, or body language.

It's easier to help Fido if we know when he's lonely, sad, afraid, or hungry. If we know what's on his mind, we can predict how he **might** act.

So how can we know what a dog is thinking and feeling? Look at its eyes, ears, face, and tail. A relaxed, happy dog raises its ears **high.** Its eyes are **bright,** and it wags its tail. Its mouth **might** hang **slightly** open.

Glossary Links
predict
snarls

On the other hand, watch out for a dog that tilts its ears back. If it raises his tail, shows its teeth, and snarls, this dog is telling you that it is **frightened.** It **might** bite to protect itself, so stay away!

Word Count: 135

 How can you tell if a dog is frightened?

❷ A Mighty Runner

As a child in Kenya, Henry Wanyoike amazed everyone with his speed as a runner. Coaches began training him to beat world records. But one tragic day, when Henry was just 21, he had a stroke and lost his **sight.** Thinking he would never run again, Henry sank into a deep depression.

Then, a doctor told Henry that being blind did not mean he could not run again. At first, Henry was afraid to try. But to his **delight,** he found that he could still run.

He tied his wrist to a guide named Joseph. Joseph ran alongside Henry. Joseph told Henry when to speed up. When Henry needed to run around an obstacle, Joseph tugged **slightly** on his wrist.

Henry became so fast that his running time broke records. In one race, he even had to drag Joseph across the finish line!

After that day, Henry decided not to let anything stand in his way!

Word Count: 155

Glossary Links
stroke
depression

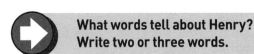

What words tell about Henry?
Write two or three words.

❶ A Wild Feast

What comes to **mind** when you think of a tasty meal? Most likely it is not a cockroach.

Even though eating cockroaches may seem like a **wild** idea, a **bold** man named Ken Edwards does just that. In fact, he is a world champion at eating cockroaches. Ken ate 36 Madagascar hissing cockroaches in one minute on a British TV show. Ken also raises odd **kinds** of cockroaches in his home.

Ken says that dining on cockroaches tastes **kind** of like having an anesthetic sprayed on the back of his throat. This taste must be the result of the smell cockroaches give off to protect themselves.

Yes, it is an odd way to gain fame. But Ken was well-known even before his crazy cockroach feast. He once stuffed 47 rats down his pants on British TV! What **wild** stunt will Ken do next?

| Word Count: 144 |

Glossary Links
champion
anesthetic

 How far would you go for fame? Tell about it.

❷ Taking Tolls (and Loving It!)

Many people ask how I like my job at the tollbooth. I tell them that my buddy Ed got me this job. And I was glad. But that feeling did not last long.

Each morning at 5 A.M., my alarm **jolts** me awake so I can get to work on time for my 6 A.M. shift.

I hate the **cold** air. It beats against the booth and chills my face. But the thing I hate the most is being alone.

"How's it going?" Ed asked me one day.

I **told** him that my job was making me crazy.

He said, "I don't **mind** it myself. The freezing **cold** keeps me awake. And I **find** empty freeways peaceful."

Glossary Links
jolts
attitude

"What about standing in the same spot all day?" I asked.

Ed shrugged. "My friend, Maggie, skips rope between **tolls.** She likes watching the stunned looks on **toll** payers' faces."

After listening to Ed, I can see how this job is **kind** of nice. My attitude has changed. Now, when I collect **tolls,** I don't **mind** it so much. I say, "Thanks, and have a nice day," and I mean it!

Word Count: 188

 How did the tollbooth operator's feelings change about his job?

❶ An Uncomplicated Request

On July 28, 1720, pirates hijacked a sailing ship carrying Irish colonists to Boston.

Unluckily, for Elizabeth Wilson, this happened just as she was giving birth to a baby. A pirate named Phillip Babb overheard the baby's cries and ran to Elizabeth's cabin.

"Lady," he said. "Is the baby a boy or a girl?"

"My babe's a girl," Elizabeth responded.

Babb said, "Then, I have an **uncomplicated** request. I will release this ship and everyone on it if you will name this baby Mary after my mother."

Elizabeth proclaimed, "Her name is Mary!"

Glossary Links
pirates
colonists

Babb kept his promise. He freed the ship and left with his men. Before leaving, he gave Elizabeth a gift of pale green silk cloth. This was for Mary's wedding dress.

Soon, Elizabeth kept her promise as well. In 1742, her daughter, Mary, was wed in a dress made with pale green silk. It was the gift from Phillip Babb.

Word Count: 153

What did Elizabeth name her baby? Tell why.

Science Nonfiction

❷ Is Cave Life Unappealing?

Some animals make their homes deep within the darkest places in a cave. These cave-dwelling animals have adapted to a lifetime in the dark.

Because a cave-dwelling animal does not see daylight, its sense of sight is useless. In fact, some cave-dwelling animals do not have eyes! But cave-dwelling animals use other keen senses. Strong senses of smell and taste take the place of sight.

Glossary Links
senses
remains

A cave-dwelling animal's diet is strongly affected by its habitat. Cave-dwelling animals do not have an **unlimited** choice at mealtimes. Green, leafy plants cannot grow in unlit caves. So a cave-dwelling animal must eat **decomposing** things such as animal remains and plant bits.

The life of a cave-dwelling animal might seem grim and **unappealing.** But the study of cave life is not **uncomplicated.** In fact, scientists find a cave-dwelling animal's life fascinating.

Word Count: 146

 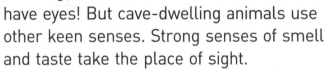

Write two facts about cave-dwelling animals.

❶ Smart Sharks

You might think that **sharks** are not **smart.** You might think that they cannot learn tasks. But did you know that in 1963 a scientist named Dr. Eugenie Clark trained **sharks** to do simple tasks?

These **sharks** lived in a **large** tank at a lab in Florida. Dr. Clark taught them to press a bell in the tank with their noses. This made the bell ring. It also let the **sharks** know they would find fish in another **part** of their tank. Some **sharks** learned this lesson in just ten tries.

Dr. Clark stopped experimenting for ten weeks. Then she set up the bell again. The **sharks** had not forgotten the lesson! Maybe **sharks** really are **smart.**

Word Count: 118

Glossary Links
scientist
experimenting

 How did this text change your opinion about sharks?

Fiction

❷ Stars in the Sky

Marcus and his mom passed the movies on their way home.

Marcus asked, "Mom, can we see a movie?"

"No, it's a school night," his mom said.

Marcus looked up at the sky. "I can't see any **stars,**" he said.

"That's because we live in the city," his mom explained. "City lights are so bright they block the **starlight.** On Friday night, we will go out to your uncle's house. You will see lots of **stars** at his place."

On Friday, they took the bus to Marcus's uncle's. While walking in the big, **dark yard,** Marcus gazed up at the sky. Millions of **stars** twinkled **far** overhead.

Glossary Links
constellation
satellite

"See that constellation?" his mom asked. "Its name is the Big Dipper. That's because it is shaped like a ladle."

"Is that a moving **star?**" Marcus pointed at a tiny light moving slowly across the night sky.

"No," his mom said. "That's a satellite."

"Wow, this is much better than a movie!" Marcus exclaimed.

Word Count: 160

 What constellation did Marcus see? Describe it.

① Artist Diego Rivera

Diego Rivera (1886–1957) began his life as an **artist.** He got his **start** drawing on the walls of his family's home. His dad, impressed with his talent, gave Diego his own space just for his **art.**

By age 10, he was taking **part** in **art** classes at night. By age 13, he became an **art** student in Mexico City.

Rivera liked making his **art** using **charcoal** pencils. But it was his bright paintings and **large** murals that got him noticed.

Rivera painted political subjects. His paintings showed problems in Mexican society as well as in daily life. He painted life as he saw it.

Glossary Links
political
society

Lots of people found his subjects **alarming.** Still, the world learned a lot about life in Mexico because of his **art.** Today, Rivera is **regarded** as one of the finest **artists** of his time.

Word Count: 138

 What subjects did Rivera paint?

❷ A Startling Find

Did you ever get an item at a **yard** sale or thrift shop and think that it might be priceless? If so, then read about the item that Michael Sparks picked up.

In **March** of 2006, Sparks was inspecting some junk that had been **discarded** in a local thrift shop. That is when he spotted an old **parchment** with the Declaration of Independence written on it. He liked it, so he paid the $2.48 that it cost.

That was quite **smart.** Sparks quickly learned that his **parchment** was one of only 200 copies of the Declaration made in 1820.

Sparks decided to sell his amazing thrift shop find for $477,650! That is quite a profit!

The man who donated the **parchment** to the thrift shop was shocked at the mistake he had made. He did not see that his **parchment** was not a fake. But he said that he is happy for Sparks.

> **Glossary Links**
> parchment
> treasure

Sparks's tale illustrates that the old saying is right. *"One man's trash is another man's treasure."*

Word Count: 169

 Explain the saying in the last sentence.

1 Within Her Reach!

When Claudia Mitchell lost **her** arm in an accident, she thought **her** life was **over.**

Little did she know that medical technology would help **her** in important ways. Mitchell got fitted with an artificial arm. This arm is set up so that Mitchell can control it with **her** brain.

After the accident, doctors saved the shoulder **nerves** that controlled Mitchell's real arm. Those **nerves** are now attached to **her** chest muscles. The **nerves** send signals that tell Mitchell's arm to move. Now, when she tries to shake a **person's** hand, she just needs to think about it!

Glossary Links
technology
limbs

"I can open jars. I can make a sandwich without my bread sliding everywhere. I can hold a big fat deli sandwich that is piled with cold cuts. There are a lot of daily tasks that I can do now," says Mitchell.

Engineers and doctors got together to invent this technology. It is part of a program funded by the U.S. **government.** Hundreds of men and women who lost an arm or leg while **serving** in the Middle East now have these amazing limbs, too.

As for Mitchell, she is thrilled! Her life has changed as a result of the help that **modern** science has **offered.** With this arm, everything is within **her** reach! Word Count: 211

How does Mitchell control her artificial arm?

Life Skills Nonfiction

❷ Making a Difference

Do you have a bit of free time and a desire to help? Would you like to make a big **difference** in your community? Then think about becoming a volunteer.

Volunteers take part in activities that can teach them job skills. And volunteering can help a **person** decide on a career path. It can **offer** volunteers chances to make friends as well.

> **Glossary Links**
> volunteer
> elderly

There are lots of ways a volunteer can help. A **person** can help cook and **serve** food at **emergency** meal programs. A **person** can plan clothing or toy drives. A **person** can help bathe dogs at animal **shelters.** Or a **person** can spend time with **elderly** people.

Volunteering is a **terrific** way to spend the day, either with family **members** or friends. But the best part of all is that it helps a **person** feel **better** about him or **herself.**

Word Count: 146

 What are some things you can do to help out in your community?

❶ A Bird Puzzle

March 27

We went on a class field trip to a farm. During lunch, I heard lots of **chirping.** Then, I discovered a little mystery. A bunch of yellow and black **birds** had landed in a dry, dusty patch of **dirt** beneath a **birch** tree. The **birds** began **squirming** in the **dirt, stirring** it up until every bird had made a **dirt** cradle.

March 28

My teacher told me those **birds** are called goldfinches. When they **twirl** in the dry **dirt,** they are taking a **dirt** bath! I do not understand how that gets them clean. I'm going to find out more about this on my computer.

March 29

I learned that lots of **birds** take dust baths in the summer. **Bird** experts **confirm** that **dirt** can clean feathers and soothe **birds'** skin. A **dirt** bath may even help the **birds** get rid of pests like lice. My little mystery has been solved!

Word Count: 155

 How does a dirt bath help a bird?

Glossary Links
cradle
soothe

Idioms

❷ Bird Talk

The word **"bird"** turns up a lot in common sayings. Read the following funny examples:

- To *"eat like a* **bird"** means to eat just a little bit.

- If something is *"for the* **birds,"** it means that it is useless. It is not to be taken seriously.

- When **"birds** *of a feather flock together,"* it means that people with common interests like spending time with each other.

- *"A little* **bird** *told me"* is used when a person does not wish to say where he or she got information.

Glossary Links
sayings
not to be taken seriously

- *"A* **bird** *in the hand is worth two in the bush"* means that it is better to keep hold of what you have and not risk it by being greedy and trying to get more.

- If a person *"kills two* **birds** *with one stone,"* that means he or she has solved two problems at the same time.

Can you think of another saying with the word **bird** in it? Give it a try. It is not just for the **birds!**

Word Count: 167

 Write a sentence using one of these sayings.

❶ Safe Web Surfing Tips

Surfing the Web can be fun and helpful. You can find useful stuff on the Web, such as movie times and news articles. But if you are not careful as you **surf** the Web, you might take a wrong **turn.** Some Web **surfing** can **hurt** you.

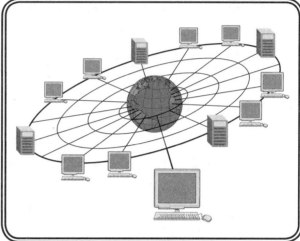

Do not give out personal information on the Web. Some Web sites use that information for bad purposes. If a Web site asks for your name, home address, phone number, or other information, ask an adult to check the site first.

Glossary Links
curb
hacked

Remember to **curb** what you say in an email. **Surprisingly,** email is not as personal as you might think. Email can be hacked into and information can be stolen.

If you are chatting and a person says something that **disturbs** you, exit the site right away. Then tell an adult. Never agree to meet someone you do not know. It is very easy for a person to pretend to be someone else. Do not trust strangers you meet on the Web.

Surfing the Web can be a fun way to spend some time. But it is important to stay safe while you **surf.** If you remember these tips, the **turns** you take on the Web will be the right ones.

Word Count: 188

 List two ways to be safe on the Web.

❷ Surfing the Pavement

Skateboarding is fun. But skaters needed a faster way to get around. The answer? Longboards!

Longboards made a big splash in the mid-1990s. This "sidewalk **surfboard**" has a longer deck than a skateboard. The deck is the part that skaters stand on. The deck might **curve** up or down. How a deck **curves** changes how the longboard handles. Decks often have graphics and stickers on them. A skater can use these to make his or her board a little bit different than others.

A longboard has wider wheels than a skateboard. Its longer deck makes it more stable. This makes it glide faster. Skaters can also make sharp **turns** better on a longboard.

Glossary Links
made a big splash
stable

Surfing the pavement is a popular pastime. In fact, races have been established with cash prizes for the winners. Look up these thrilling races on the Web. Then, maybe you can check one out!

Word Count: 148

 Why do some skaters use longboards?

Fiction

① Attack of the Spiders!

As Shereen sat down at **her terminal** in the **computer** lab, she was **surprised** to find a tiny **spider** between two **letters** on her keyboard. Then Ty found a **spider** on a **printer.** Other kids spotted **spiders** on their **computers** as well. They jumped up and down, **squirming.**

Mr. Baker looked up. "What is the problem?" he asked, **concerned.**

Shereen showed Mr. Baker the **spider** on **her** keyboard.

Glossary Links
keyboard
tarantula

"It's just a little **spider,"** exclaimed Mr. Baker.

"But they're everywhere!" the class yelled.

"These little **spiders** are harmless," a **girl** named Haley insisted. "You guys would really freak out at Buster, my **furry** pet tarantula. He's huge!"

"Some **spider** eggs must have hatched over the weekend," Mr. Baker told the class. "We can easily get rid of them."

"But don't squish them!" Haley exclaimed. **"Spiders** are useful! They eat bugs and **other** pests."

"You are right, Haley," Mr. Baker said. "But this class can do without the **computer** bugs!"

Word Count: 158

 How would you react if you found spiders in your room?

❷ Thirsty? Drink Up!

If you play a lot of sports during the **summer,** play smart. Keep your body hydrated. That means, drink a lot of water!

About 65 **percent** of a **person's** body is made up of water. **Exercise** makes our bodies heat up. Sweating is the body's way of cooling itself. But when we sweat, we lose liquids. And when we lose a lot of body fluid, we can be in **danger** of getting a heat-related illness. We might feel dizzy. We might get cramps, a rash, rapid breath, dry skin, and a fast, weak pulse as well. A heat-related illness can have harmful effects.

Doctors and coaches tell us to drink before, **during,** and **after** taking part in a sport. They say to drink at frequent **intervals** while playing, **whether** or not we feel **thirsty.**

Glossary Links
cramps
pulse

So remember, the next time you **exercise** when it is hot, drink up!

Word Count: 149

 What is your favorite summer sport? Tell about it.

❶ Glaciers in Greenland

Over the past decade, Greenland has been getting hotter. The change in Greenland's climate has changed the lifestyle of its citizens.

Climate change has melted the snow that Greenland has relied on to travel across the land. Dogsledding has become incredibly difficult.

And in the city of Ilulissat, which is 200 miles north of the Arctic Circle, a huge **glacier** is melting. The **glacier** is melting at a rate that is four times faster than in the past. The melting **glacier** has released many icebergs into the water. The large number of icebergs have led to an increase in sea levels. Icebergs also make traveling by sea more dangerous.

Glossary Links
Arctic Circle
self-sufficient

But not every change has been bad. In the past, Greenland has been a poor nation. It has had to rely on Denmark for help. But warming has made farming easier. And better crops have made the citizens richer. Greenland hopes that the money will help them solve their **social** and economic problems. They also wish to be **self-sufficient** as well. Independence from Denmark is one of Greenland's biggest goals.

Word Count: 180

 Tell two ways that climate change has affected Greenland.

❷ The Special Olympics

Eunice Kennedy Shriver came from a big family. She had nine brothers and sisters. One brother was John F. Kennedy. He became the 35th President of the United States. But Eunice's sister, Rosemary, was **special** to her as well.

Rosemary had a mental disability. But Rosemary was skilled at swimming and diving. Eunice did not want her sister's talents wasted. She thought that **special** kids like Rosemary should be able to play sports, too.

So, in 1962, Eunice began a day camp at her home. She invited 35 kids with disabilities to come. There, the kids could swim, jump, and run. And they could compete, too. The kids had a lot of fun and the camp became a big success. Eunice asked the Kennedy Foundation to help start up more camps like hers. By 1969, the Foundation helped 10,000 kids at 32 camps across the United States.

Glossary Links
disability
foundation

The new camps got the attention of Olympic **officials.** This led to the beginning of the **Special** Olympics.

In 1968, 1,000 athletes participated in the first **Special** Olympics games. Now, thanks to two **special** women, Eunice and Rosemary, millions of kids have the chance to compete and win each year.

Word Count: 197

Tell why the Special Olympics are important.

❶ Dr. Fraction's Contraptions

As a treat, our principal, Mr. Valdez, invited an exciting speaker to visit. We all paid close **attention** as Dr. Mercy Fraction showed us her many fascinating **inventions.**

Dr. Fraction explained that she had always been interested in making new and exciting things. She made her first **invention** when she was just ten. She made a fancy box that sprung open. It had a platform that came up with a cake on it when she hit a button.

Now that Dr. Fraction is grown, she invents things for a living. She showed us many strange things, such as a hat with a fan. The hat fans you when you are jogging, so you can keep cool while you are in **motion.**

Glossary Links
inventions
contraption

Then she showed us a **contraption** that closes windows from far away. Dr. Fraction said, "This **invention** helps when you forget to close the windows before leaving home and it starts raining." It was a pretty cool **invention.**

I think Dr. Fraction has one of the best jobs in the world. Maybe I will be an inventor like Dr. Fraction when I grow up.

Word Count: 184

 Describe Dr. Fraction. Write three words that tell about her.

Science Nonfiction

❷ Motion Sickness in Space

Around 60% of astronauts feel sick and dizzy during their first days in space. The **motion** sickness is a result of the need to adjust to **conditions** that are different in space than those on our planet.

On Earth, gravity gives us the **notion** of which **direction** is up and which **direction** is down. In space, astronauts are in a constant state of free fall. This makes their bodies feel as if gravity no longer exists. So, they can no longer tell which way is up or which way is down. Without a sense of **direction,** an astronaut may feel confused.

Glossary Links
gravity
nausea

While in free fall, astronauts have a hard time keeping track of the **position** of their arms and legs, despite the fact that they can see them.

This difference between what an astronaut sees and the way that he or she feels can trigger **motion** sickness. He or she might suffer from bad headaches, an inability to focus, and nausea. NASA is paying plenty of **attention** to this problem.

Word Count: 170

 How might free fall make an astronaut feel?

❶ A Model Sailor

J.D. Reddaway was just 14 when he participated in the Orange Bowl Junior Olympic Sailing Festival in 2006. Little did he know that he would finish the race a hero.

Just as the race began, a sailboat capsized and a boy fell in the water. J.D. stopped his boat to check on the child. The child began crying and said that he might be hurt.

J.D. dove in and swam to the boy's boat. The boat's ropes and **cords** were tangled up. J.D. began to **sort** out the tangle to make sure the boy was not trapped. J.D. stayed with him until help arrived. The race was postponed so J.D. could still participate.

Three months later, the United States Sailing Association presented J.D. with its National **Sportsmanship** Award. It honors those who have shown fine **sportsmanship** in the **sport** of sailboat racing.

> **Glossary Links**
> capsized
> postponed

J.D. was the youngest person to win this award.

Word Count: 151

Why did J.D. win the National Sportsmanship Award?

② A Tornado Ride

A **tornado** hurled Matt Suter more than 1,300 feet on March 12, 2006. Nineteen-year-old Matt was visiting his grandmother's trailer home **north** of Fordland, Missouri, when the twister struck.

Matt says the **storm** roared like ten jets. It made the whole trailer shake. Then the trailer tipped over. A lamp fell on Matt. It knocked him out. A 150 mile-per-hour gale hurled him into the wild black night. He rode the wind 1,300 feet before he landed on the grass.

Glossary Links
tornado
roared

No other person has ridden a **tornado** that far and survived!

It is an amazing tale, but it is a little embarrassing for Matt. All he had on when he went for his ride was a pair of boxer **shorts!** Matt was a good **sport,** however. He went on to appear on TV talk shows to discuss his wild **tornado** ride.

Word Count: 145

 Tell about a bad storm that you have been in.

❶ Funnel-Web Spiders

The funnel-web spider lives in Eastern Australia. It is an extremely deadly breed. It is also **more** likely than any other spider to attack if it is cornered.

A funnel-web spider normally forms its nest underground. It uses its nest to trap its food. It does this by weaving a silk web over the opening of its nest. Then it sits inside with its legs slightly pressing on its web. The web trembles when a tasty beetle or tiny frog walks across it. If that happens, the funnel-web spider knows it is time to race over and grab its meal **before** it gets away.

Glossary Links
extremely
explore

In hot weather or after rainstorms, male funnel-web spiders often will **explore** at night. They can get into people's homes and creep into shoes or clothing.

People understand that they can not **ignore** these toxic visitors. One nasty bite can trigger illness or even death.

So if you visit Australia, do not be surprised if you see a person shake their shoes and clothes hard **before** getting dressed! It's **more** than likely that person is on the lookout for a funnel-web spider.

Word Count: 192

You are face-to-face with a funnel-web spider. What do you do?

❷ Gold on the Seashore

You might not be surprised to find a shell along the **seashore**. But do you ever expect to find bits of gold **ore?**

In 1852, people came to **explore** Oregon's southern coast. As they **explored,** they came across gold in rivers and in beach sand. **Before** long, this discovery sparked a gold rush. Miners flocked to the coast, hoping to find **more** and **more** gold. As they did so, they formed a city named Ellensburg.

Glossary Links
ore
miners

In 1861, it rained so hard that a huge flood **wore** down the beach. The storm swept the gold out of the beach sand. The mining did not stop in local rivers, but there was no **more** chance of finding gold on the beach.

However, in 1891, Ellensburg changed its name. It became Gold Beach so no one could **ignore** the fact that, long ago, the **shore** sparkled with gold.

Word Count: 145

 What happened to the gold in the beach sand at Gold Beach?

❶ Weather Reports

It is easy to take weather **for** granted when it is nice out. But when it turns **stormy,** the weather is hard to **ignore!**

Most newspapers contain a weather **report.** It is **organized** into three **categories:** local, national, and international. A weather **report** tells the reader the **forecast.**

Local weather is probably most **important** to you. The local **forecast** will tell you if the temperature will be hot **or** cold. It will help you decide if it is best to stay in **or** go out on a specific day.

On the Web, you can find weather **information** for cities in every **corner** of the globe. For example, it might be hot and 90 degrees in Madrid, Spain. At the same time, it might be cold and 20 degrees in Nome, Alaska.

The weather is constantly changing. Pick up a newspaper or check out the Web. There you can find weather **reports for** your city—**or for** cities across the globe.

Word Count: 160

REGIONAL Weather

Tuesday, Jan. 8

Seattle 45° | 34°
Billings 34° | 17°
Salt Lake City 37° | 21°
Denver 39° | 15°
San Francisco 53° | 44°
Phoenix 60° | 42°
Albuquerque 47° | 23°
Los Angeles 59° | 44°
El Paso 54° | 34°
MEXICO

© 2008

Showers　Rain　T-storms　Flurries　Snow　Ice　Sunny　Pt. Cloudy　Cloudy

Weather Underground • AP

Glossary Links
local
forecast

 Where do you go to get the weather forecast?

Fiction

❷ A Memorable Performance

My city held a talent contest. It was **sort** of like those TV talent shows. My mom has always told me that my singing is incredible. It sends chills down her spine. So I felt it was **important** that I share this gift with others. And maybe I would become a star!

I chose a song and practiced it a lot. I sang it **morning** and night. I sang it at the park and on the street **corner.**

On the day of the contest, I **wore** my best shirt. I felt amazing. I was sure to win!

Glossary Links
chills down her spine
career

Before I went on stage, I saw my mom sitting in the back. She was planning to **record** me as I **performed.** She gave me a wave **for** good luck!

As **for** how I **performed** for the judges? Well, I will say that I did give them chills—but not the right kind. I was sad that I came in last place.

Oh well, at least I have a backup plan. My road to **glory** has not ended. Now that my singing career is over, I will start art classes. You never know, I might become the best painter!

Word Count: 196

 What is your advice to the kid in this story?

Profile

① Andrew Clements, Writer

Have you ever wondered why an object has a specific name? The **writer** Andrew Clements asked that question in his funny novel, *Frindle*.

In the novel, a boy named Nick Allen asks, "Why is a pen called a *pen*? Why can't it be a *frindle*?" In no time, kids at Nick's school begin to say *frindle* instead of *pen*. Then, the whole planet starts saying *frindle*, and the word Nick invented is added to the dictionary.

Glossary Links
publishing
managed

Writing a story that was set in a school was easy for Clements. He started his career as a **teacher.** Later, he decided to be a **songwriter.** When a friend invited him to help start a children's book publishing company, he worked as a sales **manager** and **editor.** Then he started writing his own novels.

Now, many years later, when kids ask him how he has managed to write dozens of books, he says, "One word at a time."

Word Count: 155

Invent a new word for a thing. Tell what it is. Then tell how you came up with it.

Fiction

❷ Former Track Star Becomes Swimmer

"Are you a **swimmer?**" asked Mr. Drake, the P.E. **teacher** at Cory's new school.

"No sir, I'm a **runner.** Does this school have a track team?" Cory asked. At his old school, he had set a record in the 50-yard dash. This new school had no running track, but it did have a pool.

Mr. Drake told Cory, "I will bet I can train you to swim for the swim team. We can put your athletic skills to good use. As a **beginner,** you'll start in the shallow end." Cory was not thrilled, but said he would give it a try.

Mr. Drake turned out to be a bit of a **joker.** Each day he would leap into the pool with a big splash. Cory liked Mr. Drake. And Mr. Drake was a great **instructor,** too. After just three weeks, Cory was a fine **swimmer,** and he joined the swimming team.

Glossary Links
track
athletic

A **reporter** wrote an article after Cory's first meet. The title was, "Former Track Star Becomes Top **Swimmer!**" After seeing that, Cory smiled from ear to ear!

Word Count: 179

 Why did Cory change from a runner to a swimmer?

① The Three Bears

Three bears named Benny, Kenny, and Penny lived together in a cabin. They liked to bicker constantly.

"My oatmeal is chilly," stated Benny. "I will not eat it!"

"Mine is even **chillier**," claimed Kenny.

"Mine is **chilliest**," responded Penny. "But I am not complaining." And she ate it up.

Next, it was time to clean the dishes. "My dish is **cleaner** than yours!" exclaimed Benny.

"No, my dish is **cleanest!**" stated Kenny.

"My plate is super clean, AND I cleaned it **faster** than both of you," bragged Penny.

Glossary Links
complaining
moonlight

The three bears spent so much time bickering that they spent little time tidying up their cabin.

Then, one night, an electric wire broke. The lights suddenly went dark.

"It's black in here!" whined Benny.

"This is the **darkest** night I've ever seen!" stammered Kenny.

"I have seen **darker**," Benny bragged.

"Let's go sit in the moonlight," suggested Penny.

So they did. While they sat outside, they argued over which star was **highest** in the sky, and which star was **brightest.** And they could not have been **happier.**

Word Count: 176

 What do you think the bears like to do most? Tell why.

Science Nonfiction

❷ Which Pole Is Coldest?

The North Pole and the South Pole are both incredibly cold places. But which is **colder?**

It turns out that the South Pole is a lot **colder** than the North Pole! But why is it **colder?**

Cold places get little sunlight and have very dry air. Both poles get very little sunlight. But the North Pole is located in the middle of the Arctic Ocean. The South Pole is located on the continent of Antarctica and has an elevation of 9,000 feet above sea level. So the South Pole is farther from water than the North Pole. That means its air is **drier.** That makes the South Pole **colder.**

Glossary Links
elevation
station

Still, the South Pole is not the **coldest** place on the planet. But the **coldest** place on the planet is in Antarctica as well. It is Vostok Station. It has an elevation that is over 2,000 feet **higher** than the South Pole's.

Vostok Station gets even **colder** than Earth's **highest** mountain, Mt. Everest.

Word Count: 162

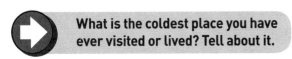

What is the coldest place you have ever visited or lived? Tell about it.

Fiction

1 That Is Some Haircut!

When Uncle Tate retired from his job **repairing airplanes,** he made his dream come true. He set up a barbershop right next to his home! And his customers love the new shop.

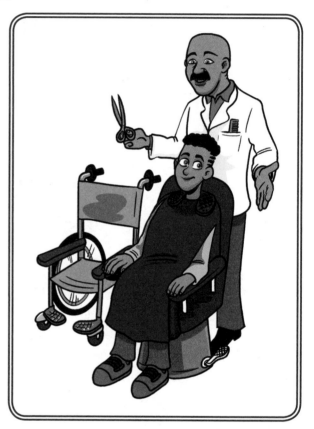

The shop has all the bells and whistles. Uncle Tate's customers sit in plush **chairs** while getting a **haircut.** They can relax and watch two different sporting events at the same time on a **pair** of flat-screen TVs. They can go **upstairs** to play chess. Or they can sit and chat over a cold drink from the snack bar. Uncle Tate even put in an elevator so his customers in **wheelchairs** can get **upstairs.**

Uncle Tate's barbershop is fantastic. And people say getting a **haircut** at Uncle Tate's barbershop makes them feel like a million bucks.

Word Count: 129

Glossary Links
bells and whistles
feel like a million bucks

Tell about a favorite shop in your neighborhood.

❷ The Story of the Chair

In ancient times, most people did not do a simple thing like sit in a **chair.** In fact, back then only kings, queens, and other leaders dared to sit in **chairs.**

Chairs raised them higher up than common people. Sitting higher up showed that a person deserved respect. Ordinary people did not begin to use **chairs** until the 16th century. Most just sat on floors, stools, chests, or benches.

The dictionary defines a *chair* as "an item of furniture made for one person to sit on." It usually has a back, legs, and maybe armrests.

Glossary Links
ancient
century

Nowadays, **chairs** come in a lot of shapes and sizes—from round to square, and sometimes even in odd shapes like hearts or hands! It is not uncommon to see **pairs** of matching **chairs** in people's homes.

So, the **chair** has come a long way. In fact, chances are you're sitting in a **chair** right now!

Word Count: 151

 Write one fact you learned from this text.

❶ A Giant Hare

Hans Wagner **shared** his prize rabbit at a rabbit show in 2006. People gathered to **stare** at the biggest **hare** they had ever seen. Wagner named his **hare** Herman.

Herman is a breed of rabbit called a "German Giant." This breed is known for its big size. But he is even large **compared** to other German Giants. At 17 pounds, he weighs about four pounds more than most German Giant rabbits! Standing on his back legs, Herman is more than 3-feet tall!

But this huge **hare** needs no special **care.** He eats the same food as most **hares**—plain green lettuce. He just eats more of it!

Wagner said that his **hare** has a mild temper. That makes Herman a "gentle" Giant.

Word Count: 123

Glossary Links
hare
breed

 Tell two facts you learned about German Giant hares.

❷ A Very Rare Bat

No mammal is as tiny as a bumblebee bat. In fact, this bat gets its name because it is as little as a bumblebee! It is also named "Kitti's hog-nosed bat" because it has a **square** nose. Biologists **compare** its nose to a pig's or hog's nose.

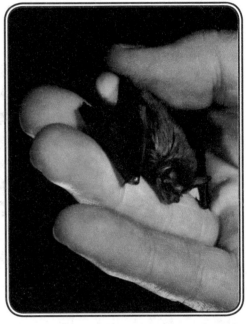

The bumblebee bat is also quite **rare.** There are only about 200 bumblebee bats alive. They live in just one place. Their habitat is a tiny part of Thailand.

Since 1974, when this bat was first discovered, people have travelled the globe to **stare** at this tiny mammal. But visitors can be bad for the bumblebee bat's **welfare.** They invade and harm the caves in which the bats sleep.

Glossary Links
welfare
fate

These bats face another problem as well. They feed on insects that gather near teak trees. But the trees in the bats' habitat keep getting chopped for lumber.

Many people are trying to **spare** the fate of bumblebee bats. They need our help. What can we do to help the bumblebee bat?

Word Count: 169

Tell two reasons why bumblebee bats are at risk.

Fiction

1 A Pair of Pears for Mr. Hill

Mr. Hill serves lunch at Tomas's school. He always has something corny to say, but it makes the kids laugh.

When Tomas came through the line without a smile on his face, Mr. Hill exclaimed, "That's a rare stare. Cheer up!"

Or he might say, "I can spare a rib today" while holding out a sparerib. But his favorite line was, "Would you like a boiled egg? It's pretty hard to beat!" Some of the kids rolled their eyes, but a lot just giggled.

Glossary Links
corny
spare

One day, Tomas had on a T-shirt with two **pears** on it. Tomas had a big smile on his face as he waited in the lunch line. He was betting that Mr. Hill would say something funny.

"Well, Tomas!" Mr. Hill exclaimed. "Now you just need a pair of pants with **pears** on the pockets to **wear** with your pair of **pears** T-shirt!"

Mr. Hill was not exactly funny, but a bunch of kids cracked up anyway. Lunch is never dull when Mr. Hill is around!

Word Count: 172

 Tell about a person who makes you smile.

❷ Where Did Bear Go?

Jeanie and Frank Flores had a dog named Bear. When Jeanie and Frank moved in 1997, Bear got lost. The I.D. tag that Bear was **wearing** had not been updated with his new address.

Jeanie and Frank put up flyers and drove along the streets by their old home. They placed ads in papers. They did not care what they had to do. Frank and Jeanie needed Bear back. Then they waited and waited.

Jeanie and Frank were scared, and waiting made them want to **tear** their hair out. But they would **swear** not to give up hope.

Six years passed. Then, one day, Jeanie saw Bear standing outside. She stared in disbelief. Then Jeanie called Bear in and wrapped her arms around him. And she began to cry.

Glossary Links
updated
flyers

Bear came back in fine shape. It seemed as if someone had taken care of him. Bear's owners may never know where he went, but they are thrilled that he is back home with them.

Word Count: 164

Tell two or three things that Jeanie and Frank did to get Bear back.

Social Studies Nonfiction

❶ Grasshopper Nightmare

The *Little House* novels, by Laura Ingalls Wilder, tell of the life of a family. Many of the tales are based on Wilder's life in America long ago. They tell of events that really happened, such as the Grasshopper Plague of 1874.

One day, Wilder's family was working in their wheat fields. Then, the sky turned black. A cloud of grasshoppers blocked the sun's light.

Suddenly, a huge grasshopper landed on the bonnet Wilder was **wearing.** Then more grasshoppers followed. **Scared,** Wilder started to run. Grasshoppers crunched under her feet.

Glossary Links
bonnet
hardships

Wilder's father made fires on the edge of his field to **scare** away the insects. But it was too late. Grasshoppers had eaten everything.

The next summer, the family discovered that the grasshoppers had laid eggs. When the eggs hatched, new grasshoppers ate up the next wheat crop.

The Wilder family was in **despair.** They had not been **prepared** for the Grasshopper Plague. It wrecked crops across several states in the 1870s.

Wilder's novels tell about hardships her family faced, such as the Grasshopper Plague. Yet, they also tell of a family that **shared** love and stayed strong together. | Word Count: 189 |

What was the Grasshopper Plague? Tell about it.

2 Cancer Scare

Brittany Leitz beamed when she became Miss Maryland in 2006. No one was **aware** of her **scary** battle with skin cancer.

In 2005, a doctor told Brittany that she had skin cancer. She got it as a result of her tanning habits. Brittany had always felt she looked better **wearing** a tan, so she went to a tanning salon up to four times a week.

Brittany suffered pain and scarring from having 25 operations in two years. But she was lucky. She survived to **share** her story!

Glossary Links
beamed
scarring

Doctors say the rate of skin cancer is increasing. This is mostly due to tanning salons. Doctors warn that tanning before age nineteen is **careless.** It increases a person's chances of getting skin cancer. People who visit tanning salons may get skin problems that are impossible to **repair.**

Brittany is dedicated to **sharing** her story. She speaks to teens in schools and in videos on the Web. She makes them **aware** of the dangers of tanning. She wants teens to know it happened to her. And it could happen to them, if they are not **careful.**

Word Count: 183

How does Brittany Leitz help others?

1 Gold Coin Mine

Back in 1890, a man discovered gold ore next to Pike's Peak in Colorado. Before long, mines popped up everywhere. "Gold Rush Fever" had struck hard and fast.

During this time, two men, Harry and Frank Woods, made a **choice** not to mine. Instead, they sold supplies to miners. Next, they invested in land. Then the men sold the land to miners for a hefty profit.

Glossary Links
profit
construct

Harry and Frank used their profit to build a town they named Victor, Colorado. As miners **joined** the town, the men began to construct a badly needed hotel. Frank and Harry hired men to dig up the **soil** to clear space for the hotel. As the workers were digging, they stumbled upon a huge surprise! Harry and Frank had struck gold!

After the hotel was finished, Gold **Coin** Mine was built directly under it. The mine has made more than a billion dollars in today's money.

Word Count: 152

 Imagine you have $1 billion. What would you do?

❷ A Car With a Voice

These days, drivers who want to **avoid** reading maps have another **choice.** Drivers can get a global positioning system, or GPS. A GPS uses satellite signals to beam digital maps and directions to drivers inside their cars.

Most GPS devices have a **voice** that will tell drivers things like, "Turn left in five hundred feet," or "Arriving at the location on the right."

For an added fee, drivers can get **pointers** on ways to **avoid** traffic jams. Or they can download the **voice** of a celebrity. Would you like to hear a famous person telling you which way to go?

> **Glossary Links**
> digital
> devices

Some people think that the extra **noise spoils** the ride. But many GPS owners like their GPS because it keeps them from getting lost. Besides, it is much safer than trying to keep your eyes on the road while reading a map!

Word Count: 142

 Would you like a GPS device? Tell why or why not.

1 Soy Milk

Some people's bodies cannot handle drinking cow's milk very well. And some people do not eat or drink anything made from animal products. For these people, **soy** milk is a healthy choice. It is also low in fats and rich in vitamins and minerals.

Soy milk was invented in China long ago. It is made by soaking **soybeans** in water and then grinding them while adding water. **Soy** milk is a mix of one part **soy** and ten parts water. This blend is heated and then filtered. Sweeteners and flavors like vanilla are also added.

Glossary Links
healthy
filtered

The resulting **soy** milk tastes a lot like cow's milk, and many people like adding it to their cereal and tea, in place of milk.

In fact, try adding tasty **soy** milk to your next drink or food in place of milk. You just might like it.

Word Count: 142

 Have you tried soy milk? Tell why or why not.

❷ Toy Time

Ask any **boy** or girl if he or she likes **toys.** Most kids will probably say "Yes!" After all, **toys** are an important part of growing up. They can also bring a lot of **joy.**

Kids can gain important skills from playing with **toys.** For example, kids can find out about construction by making a skyscraper with blocks. Playing video games helps teach thinking and problem-solving skills.

Glossary Links
construction
equipment

Balls, jump ropes, and other sports equipment can help kids stay fit. They can also teach about teamwork and how to get along with others.

Yes, **toys** can help teach new skills and keep kids fit. But the best thing about **toys** is that kids **enjoy** them!

Word Count: 115

Did you have a favorite toy or game when you were younger? Tell about it.

❶ From Disappointment to Rejoicing

Doctor Spence Silver had a **disappointing** day at work. He had just invented a glue that was not very sticky. It also never seemed to dry. This **annoyed** him. What could he do with a non-sticky, non-drying glue? Should he just **destroy** it?

Then Silver's co-worker, Arthur Fry, had an idea. Fry realized that he could put the glue on little pieces of paper and then use those sticky pieces of paper for marking his place in a book. Silver and Fry began using the self-stick notes at work. Co-workers began asking them to make more. Soon, these self-stick notes were stuck all over the office! Silver and Fry could **rejoice!** They had discovered a winner!

Glossary Links
co-worker
flop

These days, we find self-stick notes everywhere. This is a perfect example of how an invention that was first considered a flop turned into a huge success!

Word Count: 150

 Why do you think the author chose this title?

❷ Are Messes Annoying or Helpful?

So, your room is a mess and your mom is **voicing** her **annoyance.** But some experts think a little mess is not a bad thing.

For example, scientist Alexander Fleming went on vacation in 1928. He left his lab in a messy state. When he came home, he found a lab dish under the mess. The dish looked odd to him. When he peeked at the dish's contents through his microscope, he made an incredible discovery! Because of his mess, he had discovered penicillin.

Glossary Links
creativity
penicillin

Messiness may help inspire creativity as well. For example, a glance through piled-up papers on a desk might lead a person to link ideas together in a fresh way. This result might never happen if the papers were neatly filed away.

Experts also make the **point** that you can spend so much time tidying up that you may **avoid** doing other more important things.

But keep in mind that those experts were referring to little messes. If your space is so messy that you can never find things, then you have a big problem!

So messiness has its benefits. But can you convince your mom of that?

Word Count: 192

Do you think it is better to be neat or messy? Tell why.

❶ A City Rebounds

New Orleans is a city in the American **South.** It sits at the **mouth** of the Mississippi River. And it is known to many as "The Big Easy," because it is a fun city that is known for its easygoing lifestyle.

But, in late summer of 2005, New Orleans was struck by a hurricane named Katrina. Katrina's strong winds destroyed buildings and made large **amounts** of water surge into the city. The storm killed **about** 2,000 people and left tens of **thousands** more **without** homes. After the storm, the levees that were supposed to hold back the river failed. Most of the city flooded.

Glossary Links
surge
levees

Countless survivors gathered in large crowds in the downtown center, hoping to be saved. **Cloudless** skies and intense heat added to the grief. Weeks passed before order was restored.

Today, New Orleans has less than half of its former population. But it is slowly **rebounding** from its nightmare. Thanks to help from across the globe and the strength of its **proud** citizens, New Orleans is coming back!

Word Count: 172

Write two facts you learned from this text.

❷ Party Countdown

A yearly tradition in New Orleans is Carnival, a celebration that lasts several weeks. The last day of Carnival is known as Mardi Gras.

Hundreds of **thousands** of party-goers visit New Orleans each year for Carnival. A big part of Carnival is the many lavish parades. Some parades **count** on having up to 40 brightly colored floats. People ride floats, dressed up in wild costumes and masks. They throw shiny bead necklaces and other trinkets to the **ground.** The drummers in marching bands **pound** rhythmic beats. Street performers add to the exciting sights and **sounds.** They juggle, perform magic tricks, and play **loud** music.

> **Glossary Links**
> tradition
> celebration

After Hurricane Katrina struck, a **cloud** of sadness hung over this **proud** city. But city leaders voted to go ahead with Mardi Gras anyway. **Thousands** of partygoers went **south.** Mardi Gras started on time, and the city of New Orleans took a big step toward recovery!

Word Count: 151

 How did Hurricane Katrina affect Mardi Gras?

❶ Too Small to Prowl

"**Now** what is making all that racket?" Ray's grandma **frowned** as she turned on the light. "**How** am I supposed to sleep with that thing **howling** like a beast?"

Ray's grandma was lying **down** and trying to sleep. Ray climbed onto the fire escape to see what was going on.

Ray heard a dog **growling** and a cat hissing. Then it became silent. After a bit, Ray heard a sad, lonely **meow.** The sound melted his heart. Grabbing a small carton of milk, a dish, and a **towel,** he crept **downstairs** and out the back door.

Ray spotted a **brown** and black kitten **scowling** at him beside a trash can.

Glossary Links
scowling
prowling

"Did you fight off that big old dog by yourself?" Ray whispered. He stretched out his hand. The kitten sniffed Ray's hand and timidly drank a bit of milk.

"You are way too small to be **prowling** around and getting into fights like that," Ray said.

Ray carefully cradled the shaking kitten in the **towel.** He carried it back upstairs. **Meow!**

Word Count: 171

 Have you helped an animal before? Tell about it.

❷ Clowning and Krumping

Clowning and krumping are two styles of street dance. They both started in **south** central Los Angeles, California. Both styles are **renowned** for their fast movements that require strength and coordination.

Krumping looks a lot like **clown** dancing, or **clowning.** But **clown** dancers tend to use face paint more often than krump dancers do.

Both of these dance styles are still evolving. Dancers teach each other **how** to do moves that express different feelings. Typical **clowning** and krumping moves include chest-pops, stomps, and arm swings that can look like punches.

Some dancers perform at competitions. Performers **wow** big **crowds** with their talent and skills. Audiences vote for winners with their shouts and applause. Take a **bow,** dancers!

Word Count: 118

Glossary Links
coordination
evolving

Do you like dancing? Tell about it.

1 An Astounding Work of Art

The **background** story for the word *graffiti* can be **found** in ancient Rome. Back then, when a person needed to communicate with others, he or she scratched a note on a city wall. *Graffio* is Italian for "scratch."

Nowadays, graffiti means any markings made on property where it is not **allowed.** In many big cities, it can be **found** on buses, trains, streets, and **downtown** walls. This is a crime that costs taxpayers millions each year to clean up.

Glossary Links
Sistine Chapel
ceiling

But some people think graffiti is an art form. Take artist Paco Rosic, for example. He used more than 2,000 cans of spray paint to make a copy of the **renowned** Sistine Chapel painting on the ceiling of a store in Iowa.

So what makes Rosic's **astounding** graffiti art and not a crime? It is simple. He owns the old store in Iowa. Nobody has to pay to clean it up.

Word Count: 148

 Do you think graffiti can be art? Tell why.

❷ Powerful Listening Skills

Did you know that a person spends 70% of the day just listening? It takes a fair **amount** of time and practice to be a good listener.

This list of tips will help you listen well. Using them will help you remember facts you hear in class.

- After a person **announces** that he or she has something to say, focus your thinking as you listen.

  Glossary Links
  opinions
  concentrate

- Wait until a speaker has finished speaking. Only state your opinions or questions **aloud** when the speaker is finished.

- If you feel **drowsy,** try taking notes to help you stay focused. This will help you remember important points as well.

- Make eye contact with a speaker. Lean forward in your seat. Concentrate on what the person is saying.

Try these tips in school. Then see if your grades go up!

Word Count: 135

 What tips do you have for being a good listener?

① Sleepless in a Science Experiment

In 1964, teenager Randy Gardner decided to stay awake for as long as possible for a science fair project. He also hoped to set a world record for staying awake. The old record was 260 hours. For the first two days, Randy's friends helped keep him awake. Then Dr. William Dement, a sleep specialist, arrived to study Randy.

Glossary Links
science fair
specialist

Randy began closing his eyes during the third night. But Dr. Dement was **useful** in keeping Randy awake. He took Randy to an arcade. He and Randy played nearly 100 games of pinball. Randy found this **helpful** for staying alert.

At the end of the experiment, Randy held a press conference. He told reporters that he had stayed awake for 11 days by using "mind over matter." Then, after 264 hours and 12 minutes of being **sleepless,** Randy yawned. Then he shut his eyes, **grateful** to be going to sleep at last.

Word Count: 149

 How much sleep do you get each night?
When you get less sleep, how does it affect you?

❷ Fearless Badger

Which animal do you think is the most **fearless** on the planet? Snakes? Bears? Tigers? It is none of these. It is the small, carnivorous honey badger. Honey badgers got their name because they enjoy eating bee eggs and larvae. They can also withstand hundreds of bee stings!

This breed of badger has a body that is adapted for fighting. It has **powerful** jaws and razor-sharp claws. Its thick skin is so loose that it can twist around within its skin and bite any predator that grabs it by its neck. It also makes a loud rattling noise when approached.

Glossary Links
carnivorous
larvae

The badger will not hesitate to attack much larger animals, such as sheep, buffalo, and horses. These animals are **defenseless** against the world's most **fearless** animal!

Luckily, honey badgers like being alone and are rarely seen. They are **useful** in getting rid of rats and snakes. Oddly though, no one seems to want to thank them personally!

Word Count: 158

 Write two facts about the honey badger.

❶ Old Noodles

Next time you are in the **mood** for **noodles,** impress your friends with this **food** fact.

Experts have debated for a long time whether the Chinese, Italians, or Arabs invented **noodles.** In 2005, the debate was settled when archeologists found **proof.** In China, they dug up a bowl with 4,000-year-old **noodles** in it. Talk about leftovers!

Archeologists believe that an earthquake destroyed a city near that spot about 4,000 years ago. All things considered, the **noodles** were in pretty good shape. They were about 20-inches long and made from a grain called *millet.*

Glossary Links
archeologists
earthquake

The **noodles** were made a lot like the way people make them today. Grain is ground into flour. Then, water is added and mixed to make dough. Next, the dough is shaped into **noodles.** Finally, it is boiled.

Who knows what archeologists will find next? Maybe they will dig up the first pancake!

Word Count: 149

 What's your favorite noodle dish?

Science Nonfiction

❷ Space Boots

Many teens today will happily pay big bucks for a **cool** new fashion item. This is nothing new. And, sometimes, fashion trends can take a strange turn. In fact, in the 1970s, teens fell in love with **boots** that resembled the **boots** Neil Armstrong wore when he walked on the **moon.** And these fashionable **boots** were costly. But that did not stop teens from spending plenty of cash for them.

Real space **boots** cost a lot more than what most of us can afford. In fact, Armstrong's space suit cost millions! This might seem like a huge amount, but it is not when you think about what astronauts have to cope with. Space **boots** must be able to withstand contact with dust-sized meteors that speed up to 45,000 miles per hour. They must tolerate incredibly cold temperatures, as well as heat that can melt solid lead. No expense is spared to keep astronauts safe as they walk on the **moon.**

Glossary Links
fashionable
astronauts

Who knows? Maybe astronauts will one day walk on Mars. And perhaps that will start a Mars **boots** fad!

Word Count: 180

Can you think of a strange fashion trend? Tell about it.

Social Studies Nonfiction

❶ Blackbeard in the News

The *Boston* **News**-*Letter* was the first paper published on a regular basis in the U.S. It was first published on April 24, 1704.

Most of the **news** stories were about happenings in England, with just a small number of articles on local events.

But then the paper started printing a number of stories that readers began to follow. The stories reported details about the life and death of Blackbeard, one of history's most well-known pirates.

Blackbeard's real name was Edward Teach. He and his **crew** staged violent attacks on merchant ships and stole their cargo. The victims were not able to stand up against him and his **crew** for long. There is no proof, however, that Blackbeard ever killed anyone. Causing fear was his strongest weapon.

Glossary Links
merchant
cargo

Blackbeard's life ended in November of 1718. He died as violently as he lived. But for a brief time, his stories made him something of a celebrity to America's first **news** readers.

Word Count: 161

 Describe a person you enjoy reading about in the news.

Nonfiction

② News About Bigfoot

Many people believe that a strange apelike animal lurks in the forests of the U.S. Its name is Sasquatch, or Bigfoot.

But what is the real scoop? Does this large ape really exist? Nobody has ever trapped it or found its bones. But witnesses' stories about this strange animal have turned up in **news** reports for ages.

Many point to tracks of the shy ape as proof. But this proof is flimsy at best. Experts agree that most Bigfoot tracks are hoaxes. A **slew** of practical jokers have admitted that they **drew** fake tracks in the forest.

Bigfoot hoaxes have become a full-fledged business. Casts are made of his tracks and sold on the Web. Also witness accounts cannot be trusted because their stories cannot be supported with facts.

Glossary Links
flimsy
hoaxes

With so much fake "proof" and no real information, nobody knows for certain whether Bigfoot is real or fake.

Word Count: 149

 Do you think Bigfoot is real? Tell why or why not.

❶ The Musical Flute

A **flute** is a musical instrument. It is in the woodwind family. However, a **flute** is not like the other members of its family. Other instruments in this family need a reed to make music. A **flute** does not **include** a reed. It is just a **tube** that is open at both ends. The air flowing inside the **flute** creates a **tune.**

A **flute** has holes across its top. A **flute** player, or **flutist,** holds the instrument and blows air into the largest hole. The **flutist's** fingers cover and uncover the other holes while playing. The notes change as the **flutist's** fingers cover different holes.

Glossary Links
reed
mammoths

Long ago, **flutes** were made from things such as cane and bones. Some **crude flutes** were even made from the tusks of mammoths. Today, **flutes** are made of metal or wood.

Orchestras often **include** a **flute** section. **Flutes** are also **included** in many jazz and rock **tunes.** Can you think of a **tune** that **includes** a **flute**?

Word Count: 162

 Write two facts about flutes.

❷ Singing Sand Dunes

A **dune** is a large, majestic hill made of sand. Dunes can be found in the desert, near lakes and oceans, or under water.

Dunes do not sit still. Wind and water move and change the shape of **dunes.** In fact, **dunes** can move as much as 328 feet a year!

When it is hot and dry, desert **dunes** sometimes make loud whistling, booming, and roaring noises. These strange sounds often surprise visitors.

Dunes that make these sounds are called *singing sand **dunes.*** The incredible sounds are **produced** as grains of sand slide against each other. The sounds and rumbling motion made by a singing sand **dune** can last as long as 15 minutes, and can be detected as far as six miles away.

Glossary Links
majestic
clash

Explorer Marco Polo said that singing **dunes** "fill the air with the sounds of all kinds of musical instruments." He also said that the dunes sound like "drums and the clash of arms." Can you imagine sounds like these being made by sand?

Word Count: 167

 Write one fact about a singing sand dune.

1 A Jewel in Space

After seeing Earth from space, astronaut James Irwin described it as "...the most beautiful blue marble you can imagine." After Alan Shepard walked on the **moon** in 1971, he said, "When I first looked back at the Earth, standing on the **moon,** I cried." He **knew** he was looking at a **jewel** in space.

Most people never get the chance to travel to space. But thanks to photographs, we can still see Earth from space without ever leaving the ground.

The first photos of Earth were taken in 1946. The photos were **crudely** taken by a camera attached to a rocket. The rocket climbed 65 miles above Earth's surface, then fell back to the ground minutes later.

Glossary Links
international
atmosphere

Today, astronauts take photographs of our amazing planet from the International Space Station. Satellites also orbit hundreds of miles over our planet, taking incredibly crisp photos.

But the photos do more than just fascinate us. They also provide us with important information about Earth's features, **including** its atmosphere, land, and water.

Word Count: 168

Would you like to travel to space? Tell why or why not.

❷ Renew Your Look

Short on cash but need some trendy **new** clothes? Got a new **attitude** and want to show it off? By shopping for secondhand clothes, you can save cash and find **cool,** one-of-a-kind outfits.

Follow these tips to **renew** your wardrobe:

1. Check the back of the **newspaper** for local tag sales. Check the phone listings for thrift shops. These places have excellent deals on secondhand clothing and **costume jewelry.**

2. After you locate things you might like, try them on. Sizes fit everyone differently. Of course, you can always have waistbands **loosened** or hems shortened.

Glossary Links
trendy
unique

3. Next, check the clothes with care. Check that the zippers zip and that there are no stains or holes in the fabric.

4. Remember to always clean secondhand clothes when you get home.

Hunting for secondhand clothes can be thrilling! While you may come away empty-handed, there is always a chance you may find something unique and wonderful. And do not be afraid to try on **cool** vintage clothes. **Poodle** skirts or **hoopskirts** may seem old-fashioned, but who knows? You might make a past fashion trend **new** again.

Word Count: 185

Do you like shopping for secondhand clothes? Tell why or why not.

Profile

❶ Jake Farriss Gets Cooking

Jake Farriss wants you to get **cooking!** As a teenager, Jake often made tasty snacks for his pals using his own recipes. One day, Jake's teacher told the students that they could pick their own class project. Jake decided to blend his love for **cooking** with his class project. So, Jake wrote a **cookbook.**

Jake's uncle discussed Jake's class project with a few friends who worked at a publishing house. They were impressed that a sixteen-year-old could write a **cookbook.** So, they offered to take a **look** at his **book.** And then they published it!

> **Glossary Links**
> recipes
> impressed

Jake's **book,** *The Teenager's Survival **Cookbook,*** has lots of easy-to-follow recipes and kitchen hints. Jake can't understand why anyone who likes to eat would not try **cooking.** He hopes his **book** will inspire other teens to get **cooking!**

Word Count: 138

 What would you like to cook? Tell about it.

Social Studies Nonfiction

❷ Handmade Books

Before the printing press was invented in 1450, making a **book** was a difficult task. Each **book** had to be handwritten by a scribe. The scribe wrote on pages made of animal skins. A scribe had to be very careful. If he made a mistake, he had to throw away the entire page. Then he had to start a new page all over again.

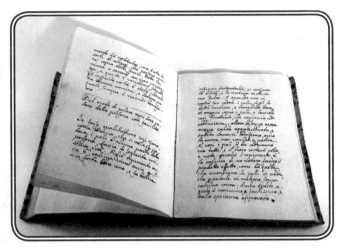

After the scribe was finished, the pages went to a person called a "red inker." The red inker wrote chapter names and titles in red ink on the pages.

Glossary Links
scribe
designs

Next, an artist added designs or illustrations to the pages. Finally, the pages went to a binder. The binder sewed the pages together. He then made a **wooden** cover wrapped with fabric or leather. This went on the front of the **book.**

Making a **book took** a very long time, so **books** cost a lot. In fact, a single **book** could cost as much as a large farm!

Word Count: 161

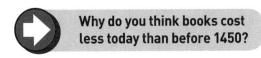

Why do you think books cost less today than before 1450?

1 Stop Pulling My Leg!

The English language is **full** of funny sayings. Sometimes the meaning of a whole phrase is different from the meaning of its words. A phrase like that is known as an "idiom."

Read the idioms below:

- "My math teacher really **pulled** *my leg* with that joke." MEANING: She likes telling silly, fake stories to tease me.

- "My dad told me to *take the* **bull** *by the horns.*" MEANING: My dad thinks I must act boldly.

> **Glossary Links**
> phrase
> block

- "This kid on my block is **full** *of hot air.*" MEANING: He enjoys bragging about himself.

- "Man, my little sister can really **push** *my buttons.*" MEANING: My sister knows just how to get me mad!

- "That runner likes to **push** *the envelope* on the track." MEANING: She tries to make herself accomplish more than seems possible.

What other idioms do you know? Share a few with a friend. Maybe you will hear a new one!

Word Count: 150

Write a sentence. Use one of the idioms from this text.

Nonfiction

❷ Pushing the Limits

The Guinness Book of World Records is a best-selling series of books. A new book has come out every year since 1955.

A world record has been set for just about everything. There are records for the smelliest socks, the tallest rose **bush,** and even the biggest collection of airline sick bags!

Other strange records:

- A Malaysian man **pulled** a 300-ton train using nothing but a steel rope clenched between his teeth.

- Two American men **pushed** a car for almost 44 miles!

- A Canadian man did 1,781 **push**-ups in one hour using the backs of his hands!

Glossary Links
series
clenched

- An Australian man has his body **fully** tattooed—even between his toes and in his mouth!

- An American woman has the longest fingernails in the world. Each nail is at least two-feet long. That is almost 25 feet in total!

Word Count: 141

 Why do you think people try to set records?

① Cook, the Ten-Foot Rookie

Cook is a **rookie.** He is **looking** forward to a career with the New York City Police Department. But he will need to put his best **hoof** forward to do that! If he makes it into the force, Cook will be one of only twenty horses chosen from a total of 1,500 horses.

But for now, Cook must **fulfill** three to six months of training. He must **push** his limits each day. But the **outlook** is **good** that Cook will end up with a job on the police force. Then he may get a new name. Most NYPD horses are given the name of a fallen New York City Police Officer. It is a real honor.

Glossary Links
rookie

honor

In New York City, police horses are known as "Ten-**Foot** Cops." New Yorkers are very proud of their ten-**foot** cops. And Cook has an important job ahead of him.

Word Count: 147

Write two facts you learned about police horses.

Social Studies Nonfiction

❷ Wooden Shoes

Klompen are interesting-**looking wooden** shoes. They are a bit like the modern clogs we wear now. Klompen were worn in the Netherlands for hundreds of years. And some people still wear klompen today.

Klompen are made from hollowed out pieces of hard **wood,** like birch or willow. They can be decorated with carvings or brightly colored paint.

Glossary Links
Netherlands
cushy

Wood has long been used for making **footwear.** Ancient Egyptians and Greeks wore **wooden** sandals. Before streets were paved, roads and paths were made of dirt. The paths frequently became muddy. So rich people would put **wooden** shoes over their fancy slippers to keep their feet clean and dry.

Can you imagine **pushing** your feet into hard **wooden** clogs and hiking around in them all day long? Klompen may be sturdy, but they are NOT **cushy.**

"Klompen" sounds like "clomp" in English, which means "to walk noisily." That is exactly how **footsteps** sound in **wooden** shoes!

Word Count: 154

 What materials are your shoes made from?

❶ It's the Law

Everyone knows it is against the **law** to commit a crime. But some **laws** are stranger than you might think.

Check out the following unusual **laws** from all over the United States.

- In Pennsylvania, it is illegal to sit down while using a hose to water your **lawn.** It is also illegal to sing in the bathtub.

- In Florida, you are not allowed to sing in public if you are wearing a swimsuit.

Glossary Links
illegal
outdated

- In Connecticut, it is against the **law** to walk across a street on your hands.

- In California, you can be fined for entering a movie theater within four hours of eating garlic.

- In Oklahoma, you can be fined, arrested, or jailed if you make ugly faces at a dog.

- In Nevada, it is illegal to drive a camel on the highway.

Keep in mind, many of these **laws** were **drawn** up a long time ago. Life was different back then. These outdated **laws** show us how much times have changed.

Word Count: 163

 Write two or three laws you might like to create.

❷ All About Straw

Straw is the dry part of a plant. It is what is left over after grains such as wheat, rice, and oats have been harvested. But **straw** is not something to just throw away. It can be recycled and reused in lots of ways.

For example, farmers combine **straw** with hay to feed their animals. But even after all the animals have been fed, there is still a huge amount of **straw** left over.

Glossary Links
harvested
recycled

The following is a list of some of the things **straw** can be used for.

- **Straw** can be used to make hats and baskets.

- **Straw** is used to make a fuel for cars that is cleaner than gas.

- **Straw** is used to make rope, paper products, and packing materials.

- **Straw** is used when growing foods like strawberries and mushrooms because it makes the soil rich. It also stops weeds from growing.

Word Count: 145

 Pick an everyday item. Tell two or three new ways you could recycle it.

① Author and Baseball Fan

Stephen King is the **author** of over 50 best-selling horror novels. His novels are known for gloomy settings and **haunting** details. He has a way of making common objects, such as cars and diners, seem creepy and sinister. Readers around the world **applaud** King's talent for providing thrills and chills.

Many people know that Stephen King is an **author.** What people might not know is that King is also a huge baseball fan. He became a fan of the Boston Red Sox as a child—long before he **launched** his writing career. King attends Red Sox games as frequently as he can.

> **Glossary Links**
> sinister
> passion

In his book *The Girl Who Loved Tom Gordon*, King combined his passion for baseball with his gift of writing horror stories. He wrote about a little girl who gets lost in the woods. To comfort herself, she plays radio broadcasts of Red Sox games. She pretends that former Sox pitcher Tom Gordon is keeping her safe.

King has also acted in a film about baseball and owns a baseball stadium in Maine. It's hard to say which King is more passionate about, his love of writing or baseball. Luckily, he has the time and the talent to enjoy both.

Word Count: 203

 Do you like reading scary stories? Tell why or why not.

❷ Launching Into Flight

Shaun's dad had finally agreed to get him a hang-gliding lesson for his sixteenth birthday. Shaun's little brother, Drew, had tagged along to watch. Shaun looked nervously at the ground from the top of the cliff. "You are going to chicken out!" **taunted** Drew.

"I bet you won't even **launch** the hang glider," Drew added.

The hang-gliding instructor, Paula, scolded Drew. "Shaun will do just fine. I have shown a lot of people how to hang glide. I take many **precautions.** Nobody has ever gotten hurt!"

Paula strapped herself into the glider's harness with Shaun. She would fly by Shaun's side.

Glossary Links
precautions
harness

"Ready?" asked Paula.

"Ready as I will ever be," replied Shaun.

On the count of three, Paula and Shaun ran to the cliff's edge and jumped, **launching** the hang glider. The air lifted them up, and away they went!

"Way to go!" Drew called from down below. Dad and Drew **applauded** Shaun's bravery.

Word Count: 156

Write two or three sentences about a time you overcame a fear.

Science Nonfiction

❶ Crazy Rainfall

Yes, **rainfall** is normally made up of water. But very strange things have **fallen** from the sky **all** across the globe.

During the 1980s, kernels of corn rained down upon a Colorado town. Oddly, there were no cornfields located close to the town.

In May of 1981, thousands of live tiny green frogs rained down on a town in Greece.

In July of 2001, residents in India saw a strange kind of **rainfall.** The rain was red. Many citizens thought it might be blood!

Glossary Links
theory
meteors

In December of 2006, thousands of dead birds fell from the sky over Western Australia.

So what caused these strange events? One theory is that **small** tornadoes swept up the corn and frogs from other places. Then they dropped the objects down on the towns. Some think that poisons killed the birds. Some think that meteors or pollution may have caused the red rain.

In other words, nobody really knows what caused these events. **Chalk** it up to another strange mystery.

Word Count: 165

**Imagine you are at one of the events in this story.
Write a paragraph that describes what happens.**

Science Nonfiction

❷ Don't Call a Wasp a Bee!

Do you know the difference between a **wasp** and a bee?

At first glance, they look very similar, and we usually **call** them both "bees." Both are insects with six legs, two sets of wings, and a body that is separated into three segments. Both have stingers. And they both help humans, but in different ways.

Now, read about how bees and wasps are different.

Honey Bees	Wasps
• live in hives made of beeswax	• live in nests made of paper
• are not very aggressive, and do not usually attack unless provoked	• are aggressive, and may attack even if they are not provoked
• females sting once and then die	• females sting again and again
• are hairy	• are smooth and a bit shiny
• eat nectar and pollen, and make honey	• eat other insects, meat, nectar, pollen, and sweets
• build hives in enclosed spaces such as hollow trees and holes in **fallen** branches	• build nests in hollow trees, between **walls,** or underground
• help humans by pollinating plants and producing honey and beeswax	• help humans by pollinating plants and eating pests, such as flies

Word Count: 180

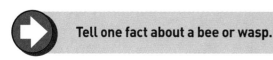
Tell one fact about a bee or wasp.

Glossary Links
segments
pollen

❶ A Flawless Player

On April 14, 1947, a **baseball** player named Jackie Robinson made history. Robinson played for the Brooklyn Dodgers. That day was his first day in the big leagues. It was also a first for **all** African-American athletes.

Born in 1919, Robinson **always** excelled at sports. In 1943, he joined a black **baseball** team called the Kansas City Monarchs. At that time, blacks and whites did not play on the same teams.

The major leagues had no written **law** against black players. Yet, teams had maintained the "color line" for about sixty years.

Branch Rickey managed the Brooklyn Dodgers. He hated **baseball's** whites-only policy. In 1945, he asked Robinson to **audition** for his team. Rickey knew Robinson could play. More importantly, he knew Robinson was brave enough to ignore the racist remarks he might get.

Glossary Links
excelled
color line

Robinson's first year with the Dodgers was difficult. Fans and players **taunted** him. Even teammates complained about playing with him. Robinson stayed cool and ignored them **all.** By season's end, he led the league in batting and stolen bases, and was voted Most Valuable Player.

In 1951, 13 more black players had joined the major leagues. Robinson had broken **baseball's** color line forever.   Word Count: 199

 How did Robinson break the color line?

❷ Watch, Read, and Applaud

Do you **always** watch films that are made in English? Or do you sometimes watch films in which the actors speak another language?

Most films shown in the United States are in English. However, lots of films from around the globe are made in different languages. There is even an award handed out to the best foreign-language film each year.

Do you think it might be **awfully** hard to understand a foreign film? It is not! That is **because** the lines that the actors speak appear **automatically** in English at the bottom of the screen. These printed sentences are **called** subtitles.

Glossary Links
foreign
automatically

Of course, actions, such as dancing or **falling** down, need no subtitles. Most people **also** understand facial expressions, such as smiles or **yawns.** Sounds, such as car horns or ticking clocks, do not need subtitles, either.

To understand a foreign-language film, see it, read it, and then **applaud** it. Seeing a foreign film can be like taking a trip to an exotic place without ever leaving home!

Word Count: 170

 Write two or three things about your favorite film.

❶ Subways Move Us

Morning, **midday,** and well past midnight, you will see people riding on subways. These underground rail systems provide public transportation for the planet's biggest cities. They also provide a fast, cheap way for people to travel. On the subway, people can get from **midtown** to the outer **suburbs** for just a few bucks or less.

The world's first **subway,** called "The Underground," opened in 1863 in London, England. The first **subway** in the U.S. opened in Boston in 1897. Now, more than 30 U.S. cities operate **subways.**

Inspired by underground travel, artists have made **subways** the subject of dances, films, and songs. Billy Strayhorn's jazz song, "Take the A Train," is about a New York City **subway** line. Well-known musicians Duke Ellington and Ella Fitzgerald made the song into one of the most famous tunes of the 20th century.

Word Count: 140

Glossary Links
transportation
midtown

What kind of public transportation is in your city or town? Tell about it.

Fable

❷ Three Pigs in the Suburbs

When the three little pigs moved out to the **suburbs,** the first one plunked down a huge sum for a split-level straw house. The second pig bought the **midsized** wooden home next door. The third pig decided he could not afford to buy a home. So he **sublet** the small house made of bricks around the corner.

Around **midnight** one evening, a wolf jumped on the **subway** near his apartment in **midtown.** He rode out to where the pigs lived.

Of course, he had no problem blowing down the straw house. And it was not hard to knock down the wooden house, either. But he had misjudged the brick house's strength.

Glossary Links
plunked down
sublet

He huffed and puffed so hard that it caused him to fall down. He tumbled head-over-paws and landed in a slimy fish pond!

The third pig invited the other pigs to move into his quaint little home and help share the rent. And the wolf learned his lesson and did not bother those pigs again.

Word Count: 169

 Would you rather live in a city or the suburbs? Tell why.

Profile

❶ A Tasty Mistake

Did you know that the potato chip was invented by **mistake?**

The story goes like this: In 1853, a chef named George Crum was cooking at a fancy restaurant in upstate New York.

One night, a diner sent a plate of French fries back to the kitchen. He complained that the fries were too thick and soggy. He also claimed that they lacked salt. Crum **disagreed,** but he tried to make the customer happy. He cooked thinner, saltier fries. Yet, the man still **disliked** them.

Now Crum felt angry. He decided to annoy the fussy customer. Crum fried paper-thin potato slices and put lots of salt on them. These fries were too thin and crisp to eat with a fork. Surely, the customer would dislike them. But Crum **misjudged** the picky eater. The man loved them! Other diners asked for Crum's potato chips, too.

Crum soon realized he'd invented a fantastic food. He later started his own restaurant that served potato chips.

> **Glossary Links**
> soggy
> picky

Word Count: 163

 What kind of a man is George Crum?
Write two or three words that tell about him.

❷ A Disappearing Dog Leads to Discovery

In 1874, Elijah Davidson, a hunter, discovered the Oregon Caves by accident. His **misbehaving** dog had chased after a bear and **disappeared** down into a dark hole. Davidson was hesitant to enter the cave and disturb an angry bear. But he lit a few matches and went in to save his dog.

Davidson had **misjudged** the size of the cave. It was much bigger than he expected. He was also **dismayed** when his flame blew out and left him in darkness. A **miscalculation** could have led to tragedy. But luckily, he found his way out. And soon, his dog did too.

Glossary Links
hesitant
dismayed

The caves that Davidson had stumbled upon are now known as the Oregon Caves. Visitors travel from far away to see the amazing cave formations. In the past, visitors **mistreated** the caves, even carving their names into the walls. Now, more care is taken. Guides forbid visitors from touching the cave walls. And the caves are better protected.

Word Count: 160

 How did Elijah Davidson find the Oregon Caves?

❶ Sports and Smoking: A Losing Combination

Smoking and sports do not mix. Why are they a bad **combination?** The **explanation** is simple. Smoking decreases the **circulation** of blood through the body.

Cigarette smoke has gases that hurt the blood's ability to carry oxygen. They make the heart pump faster. So when a person inhales cigarette smoke, his or her heart rate increases!

A faster heart rate means that less air is getting to the lungs. The blood vessels also get smaller and tighter. This affects **circulation** even more. A **combination** of rapid heart rate and less **circulation** makes it harder to breathe.

Glossary Links
oxygen
addictive

And this means that an athlete who is a smoker will not be able to keep up with a nonsmoking athlete. Worse still, the earlier a person starts smoking, the more his or her body will be damaged. Just like other drugs, cigarettes are addictive, disgusting, and deadly!

The **decision** to smoke or not smoke should be simple. Make the winning choice and stay far away from cigarettes.

Word Count: 167

 Give two reasons why smoking is a bad idea.

❷ Let the Celebrations Begin!

Need to make a **decision** about where to go on your next **vacation?** Then check out these real-life wild and wacky **celebrations:**

- *Garlic Festival in Gilroy, California:* Bring your mouthwash! You can taste foods with lots of garlic, including garlic soup, garlic pie, garlic chocolates, and garlic ice cream.

- *Cow Painting Festival in Luxembourg:* Here, you can see metal, wooden, and concrete cows with **decorations** by artists with lively **imaginations!**

> **Glossary Links**
> Luxembourg
> concrete

- *La Tomatina in Spain:* Join in a huge food fight, as crowds throw 90,000 pounds of tomatoes at each other.

- *Cooper's Hill Annual Cheese Rolling in England:* See athletes risk broken bones and bruises in a **competition** to race against a block of cheese as it rolls down a hill.

- *Moose Dropping Festival in Alaska:* Start a **collection** of jewelry made from moose droppings! Then watch out for moose droppings as they're thrown from hot-air balloons.

Word Count: 148

 Which celebration sounds the strangest to you?

Profile

❶ America's Incredible Teen Inventor

People may not know his name, but he is **responsible** for one of the most **recognizable** inventions in history! Philo Farnsworth invented the first electronic television set.

Philo grew up poor in a log cabin in Utah. In 1920, when he was just 14 years old, he gazed down at the lines made by a plow on a field. Suddenly, he saw the lines in a new way.

Glossary Links
transmitted
royalties

Amazingly, the lines gave Philo an idea of how television might work. Maybe images could be scanned and transmitted line by line. In 1927, Philo used this idea to build his first television set.

A few years later, a big electronics company claimed that *their* inventor had made the first television set. Philo decided to sue.

During the trial, his high school science teacher provided a **valuable** piece of evidence. He showed a sketch for Philo's television system that Philo had drawn when he was just 14.

The judges found Philo's story **believable.** Philo won his lawsuit against the huge company. After that, he received royalties on each television set sold.

Word Count: 179

 Imagine Philo Farnsworth is still alive. What would you ask him? Write two or three questions.

❷ Simply Unbelievable!

Have an idea for an invention that could change the world? The inventors of these **unbelievable** gadgets thought they did. Check out their ideas for crazy gadgets:

- A smell recorder that records smells and plays them back later. Store the **memorable** scent of your favorite food, soap, or flower and smell it any time!

- A lawn mower that hooks up to the back of a kid's tricycle. Get your five-year-old sister to mow the lawn!

- A banana case that keeps a banana **edible.** Prevent that banana from getting crushed in your backpack!

Glossary Links
gadgets
edible

- A hair-cutting machine that has a number of styles programmed into it. Get an **unforgettable** and trendy haircut without leaving home!

So what do you think? Are these gadgets **reasonable, sensible,** or totally useless? You can decide.

Word Count: 132

 Tell about an idea for an invention.

❶ History of the Bicycle

Most kids know how to ride a **bicycle.** But do you know the history of **bicycles?**

A kind of cycle was invented in France in the 1700s. A toymaker put a wheel on the bottom of a wooden horse. To ride this contraption, a child sat on the horse and pushed with his feet. Since the horse had just one wheel, it was really a **unicyle.**

Later, in 1817, a German inventor made a **bicycle** with two wheels. But it had no pedals. He used the **bicycle** to glide down the street. Even without pedals, it was faster than walking.

Glossary Links
vehicle
terrain

Over the next few decades, inventors made new kinds of **bicycles** and a **tricycle.** A **tricycle** is a three-wheeled vehicle that little kids ride.

The first modern **bicycle** was invented around 1863. This bike had pedals like the bikes we see today. But inventors did not stop there. Today, you can get a bike for riding city streets, for bouncing over rocky terrain, or for racing at amazing speeds. There is a **bicycle** for wherever you may go.

Word Count: 178

 What changes would you make to today's bicycles?

❷ Thrilling Triathlons

A **triathlon** isn't just one race—it's three! People who compete in **triathlons** are called **triathletes**.

In a **triathlon**, the **triathletes** swim first. Then they **bicycle.** Last, they run. Some people consider them the very best athletes. They must excel at three sports. That means they spend **triple** the time training.

Most **triathletes** don't wear just one **uniform.** They quickly change outfits between events. After a **triathlete** swims, he or she might exchange a wetsuit for **bicycle** shorts. Then, he or she might switch to running shorts.

The biggest **triathlon** on the planet is called "the Ironman." Each year, the best **triathletes** take part in this brutal race. They swim 2.4 miles in crashing waves. They **bicycle** 112 miles up steep hills. And they must finish the race by running 26.2 difficult miles.

Liquids, snacks, and an unbeatable sense of pride await the athletes at the finish line.

Glossary Links
excel
brutal

Word Count: 147

 How might triathletes feel as they cross the finish line? Write two or three words.

1 Autograph or Autopen?

Have you ever gotten a **photograph** with an **autograph** on it? If so, you probably believed that a celebrity took time to sign it.

Think again. A machine might have written on that photo. That's right. That "handwritten" autograph might have been made by an **autopen.** An **autopen** is a machine that writes **autographs.** It is made up of a fake hand and a real pen that write things **automatically.**

Glossary Links
handwritten
automatically

How can you tell whether an **autograph** is real or fake? To detect a fake **autograph,** ask the following questions:

- Does the **autograph** look a little shaky?
- Do the curved letters look scratchy?
- Is there a little ink dot at the beginning or end of the **autograph?**
- Do two or more of the same person's **autographs** look exactly alike?

Did you say "yes" to one or more of those questions? If so, then an **autopen** probably made the **autograph!**

Word Count: 149

Whose autograph would you like to have? Tell why.

2 Autobiographies and Biographies

A **biography** is a book about a person's life. Maybe you have checked one out at the library.

Usually, authors write **biographies** about well-known people, like boxer Muhammad Ali. Sometimes, authors write **biographies** about themselves. A book in which an author writes his or her own life story is called an **autobiography.**

Most **biographies** include **photographs** of the subject. But a **biography** about a person who lived long ago might not. **Photography** had not yet been invented.

A **biography** about a person from the distant past might include a portrait. A *portrait* is a likeness of a person. It can be a drawing or a painting that shows readers what the subject looked like. They can also help readers see how the subject lived.

Whose **biography** might you like to read?

Word Count: 131

Glossary Links
subject
likeness

Write the first paragraph of your autobiography.

❶ Cuban Import Goes Bananas!

In 1804, Captain John Chester's ship **imported** Cuban bananas to the United States.

As he entered New York's **seaport,** Chester could not have **predicted** what would happen next with his tropical fruit. Imagine his dismay when no one bought his bananas. The reason? Nobody, except for sailors, had ever even seen a banana. People had no idea what a banana was for! So the entire load of bananas rotted.

Glossary Links
produce
pushcarts

In 1830, another shipper **imported** bananas. This time, produce sellers bought them to sell from pushcarts. People understood what a banana was when they saw it next to other fruits.

But, because bananas were still so rare and costly, they were eaten only at very special events such as weddings. But by 1905, bananas were so common and cheap that they were enjoyed by the rich and poor alike. Now, bananas are America's best-selling fruit.

Word Count: 145

 Why didn't people buy bananas from Captain John Chester?

Profile

❷ Important Figures in Fashion

Levi Strauss arrived at a **seaport** in New York City in 1847. He came from Germany. He was just 18 years old. To make cash, the immigrant teen sold fabric around the city.

Strauss soon began hearing **reports** about California's Gold Rush. In 1853, he sailed to San Francisco to get in on the action. While he did not find gold, he did begin to sell lots of fabric. He made and sold pants, too.

Strauss used a sturdy **imported** cotton called denim to make his pants. He sold denim pants to gold miners. It was **important** for them to wear pants that could withstand harsh conditions.

Glossary Links
immigrant
rivets.

In 1872, Strauss joined forces with a tailor named Jacob Davis. Davis had invented a new way to make work pants. He used metal rivets to strengthen the pockets and zipper area. For the fabric, he used denim that he ordered from Strauss.

Davis and Strauss formed a company together. They began to make denim pants called "jeans." Nobody **predicted** it. But 160 years later, jeans are still popular. Davis and Strauss invented a style that has never gone out of fashion.

Word Count: 189

 Why do you think jeans are still popular today?

❶ Mt. St. Helens Erupts!

Mount St. Helens is a volcano in Washington State. On May 18, 1980, it **erupted.**

A huge earthquake sparked the **eruption.** The quake caused the north face of the volcano to crumble, leaving a mile-wide crater in its place. An avalanche of rock roared down the mountain. The avalanche destroyed nearly 230 square miles of forest land.

At the same time, a huge cloud of volcanic ash rose thousands of feet into the sky. It deposited ash in 11 states. Hot lava flowed from the top of the volcano. It kept flowing for nine hours.

Glossary Links
crater
avalanche

By the time the **eruption** ended, it had killed 57 people. It had destroyed bridges, roads, railways, and homes. It had caused more **destruction** than any other volcanic **eruption** in U.S. history.

Will Mount St. Helens **erupt** again? Minor eruptions happen fairly often. Experts monitor the volcano's activity. They look for signals that a major **eruption** is brewing. If a big **eruption** seems likely, experts will tell local residents to be prepared. They will provide **instructions** that **prescribe** the steps for escaping the disaster.

Word Count: 180

Imagine you are a news reporter. You see Mt. St. Helens erupt. What might you say on the news?

❷ Deadly Destruction

The Super Outbreak of April 3–4, 1974, is the largest outbreak of tornadoes on record. During an 18-hour time span, 148 twisters struck 13 states in the South and Midwest. Six twisters ranked F5 on the tornado scale. An F5 is the largest and most destructive form of tornado.

The outbreak was one of the biggest disasters in U.S. history. Its path of **destruction** stretched for 2,500 miles. Tornadoes killed 330 people and harmed 5,484 more. In Indiana, 27 schools were damaged or destroyed. Luckily, the twisters hit in the late afternoon, after students had left.

Glossary Links
outbreak
disasters

The twisters left behind horrible **destruction.** But they also left important evidence about how tornadoes act. They showed that some common myths were untrue. People believed that a tornado would not go up or down a steep hill, for example. They believed that twisters would not hit a spot where major rivers meet. But the twisters of 1974 did all of those things.

After the outbreak, experts gathered information and **descriptions.** They used it to prepare for the next big tornado. Engineers studied the flattened schools in Indiana. Then, they **constructed** new schools that could better withstand storms and protect students. Because of evidence left by the outbreak, we can stay safer when twisters strike.

Word Count: 214

 How could you prepare for a major storm?

❶ An Invisible Force

What lies between the stars? It may look like nothing. But astronomers say that the space between stars is more than just empty space.

Astronomers think this space is filled with **invisible** matter called "dark matter." We cannot see it because it produces no light.

But astronomers still think dark matter exists. They say the **evidence** lies in the way that galaxies hang together.

It is hard to tell from Earth. But galaxies and stars are in constant motion. They rotate extremely fast. In fact, they go so fast that they *should* fly apart. The stars should fly out of their galaxies. But an **invisible** force holds them together.

Glossary Links
astronomers
galaxies

Experts say that force is dark matter. They say dark matter has its own gravity. Its gravity pulls on stars and keeps them together. So, what is in dark matter? It might include gases, planets, and old stars that don't produce light. But so far, experts don't know for sure.

A project is underway to map the dark matter in two distant galaxy clusters. Experts will use photos from the Hubble Space **Telescope** to make the map. They hope this map will shed light on dark matter!

Word Count: 196

 Why do experts think dark matter exists?

Profile

❷ A Saxophonist Supreme

John Coltrane (1926–1967) is a giant of American jazz. This **saxophonist** and composer recorded and produced more than 50 albums. He worked with many of the best jazz musicians of the last century.

Coltrane grew up in High Point, North Carolina, playing horn, clarinet, and alto **saxophone**. During World War II, he served in the Navy Band in Hawaii. After the war, he settled on the East Coast. He began playing tenor **saxophone.** Later, he switched to soprano **saxophone.**

Glossary Links
composer
critics

Jazz historians credit him with developing a brand-new style of playing **saxophone**. They say he reshaped modern jazz. Critics regard his 1964 album, *A Love Supreme,* as one of the most important jazz albums in history.

Today, collectors will pay large amounts of cash for one of his autographs. His photo appeared on a 1995 postage stamp.

But Coltrane's biggest gift is his music. Jazz radio stations still play it. Fans can see and hear him play in **video** clips. Music students and professional jazz artists still love to play his compositions.

Word Count: 173

What kind of music inspires you? Tell about it.

Summary of Text Elements

▶ Below is a list of the sound-spelling correspondences and high-frequency words introduced in each text. Have students refer to this list as they read the texts.

Text Title	Targeted Sound-Spelling or Element	Previously Taught High-Frequency Words
Series 1		
Sam, p. 9	*m: am*	
Text Message, p. 9	*m: am*	
Ssssssnake!, p. 10	*s*	
Stan's Bad Day, p. 10	*s*	
Get Up, Nat!, p. 11	*t: Nat*	
Stan's Day, p. 11	*t: at, sat, Stan*	
Nan Tricks Ann (Part 1), p. 12	*n: Ann, Nan*	
Nan Tricks Ann (Part 2), p. 12	*n: Ann, Nan*	
Ant and Man?, p. 13	**Short a:** *an, ant, man, mat, tan*	*a*
A Man, p. 13	**Short a:** *man, sat*	*a*
Sap on a Cap!, p. 14	*p: cap, pan, sap, tap*	*a*
A Map Nap?, p. 14	*p: map, pats, taps*	*a*
Cat Spat, p. 15	*c: can, cat*	*a*
At Camp Sacnac, p. 15	*c: camp, can, cap*	*a*
Nat and a Cab, p. 16	*b: bam, cab*	*a*
Brant at Bat, p. 16	*b: bat*	*a*
Pam, a Cat, a Rat, and a Bat, p. 17	*r: rat*	*a*
No Rest for a Rat, p. 17	*r: rat*	*a*
A Band Jams, p. 18	**Ending -s:** *cans, pans, raps, snaps, taps*	*a*
Sam's Maps, p. 18	**Ending -s:** *camps, maps, scans, stamps*	*a*

Text Title	Targeted Sound-Spelling or Element	Previously Taught High-Frequency Words
Series 2		
Bill's Packing List, p. 19	**Short *i*:** *mitt, pic*	
Homework Fibs?, p. 19	**Short *i*:** *in, it, rip*	*has*
Dad and Dibs, p. 20	***d*:** *bad, did, mad*	*my, the*
The Bad Rap on Bats, p. 20	***d*:** *bad, mad, rid, sad*	*are, has, the, you*
Fans for Sale, p. 21	***f*:** *fan, fans, fit*	*are, has*
Fast Fins, p. 21	***f*:** *fast, fins*	*he, the*
Ham in a Can, p. 22	***h*:** *ham*	*this*
Frank's Big Hit, p. 22	***h*:** *hat, hits*	*the*
Kip's Kit, p. 23	***k*:** *kid, kit*	
Kam's Pants, p. 23	***k*:** *kit*	*the*
Top Mop Hits the Spot!, p. 24	**Short *o*:** *cannot, dot, mop, not, spots, top*	*the, this, you*
Dot and Spot, p. 24	**Short *o*:** *lot, nonstop, not*	
Late at the Lab, p. 25	***l*:** *lab, lid, lifts*	*the*
Lil's List, p. 25	***l*:** *lid, list*	*this*
Rod and His Sax, p. 26	***x*:** *box, fix, sax, six*	*he, the*
Ann and Max, p. 26	***x*:** *box, fix, six*	*are, the, this*
Yackity Yack!, p. 27	***-ck*:** *docks, kick, packs, rocks, sacks, socks, tack*	*you*
Stinky Socks, p. 27	***-ck*:** *ick, kicks, picks, sick, socks*	*he, my*

Summary of Text Elements continued

Text Title	Targeted Sound-Spelling or Element	Previously Taught High-Frequency Words
Series 3		
Slippery Stan, p. 28	**s-Blends:** *slick, slips, spots, stands, stop*	*he, the*
Colin the Slob, p. 28	**s-Blends:** *slob, spills, spits, stack, stick, stink, stop*	*he, of, to*
All-U-Can-Fit Tent, p. 29	**Short e:** *bed, red, tent*	*that, the*
Which Sled Wins?, p. 29	**Short e:** *men, red, sled, ten*	*the*
Jen Jets!, p. 30	**j:** *jam, jets, jock*	*to*
Jed's Jam, p. 30	**j:** *jam, job*	*this, to*
The Web, p. 31	**w:** *wax, web*	*of, the, to, you*
Cat in a Well, p. 31	**w:** *well, well's, went, wet*	*the, to*
Tuck and the Tub, p. 32	**Short u:** *jumps, just, mud, pup, runs, suds, tub*	*the*
Sunny Side Up, p. 32	**Short u:** *bus, but, cup, just, luck, muffin, stuff, truck, up*	*are, of, that, they, to*
Got Ya!, p. 33	**g:** *jog, legs, tag, tags*	*are, he, she, to*
Peg and the Bug, p. 33	**g:** *big, bug, bugs, digs, dog, get, jogs, rug*	*he, of, that*
Say Yes!, p. 34	**y:** *yak, yams, yell, yes, yet, yum*	*of, that, the, you*
Yuck!, p. 34	**y:** *yams, yell, yes, yet, yuck*	*are, do, me, what*
Man With a Van, p. 35	**v:** *van, vest, vet*	*are, of, the, to, you*
A Trip to the Vet, p. 35	**v:** *van, vest, vet, visit*	*she, the*
Zeb's Gift, p. 36	**z:** *zest, zip*	*he*
Zip Up the Bucks!, p. 36	**z:** *zip, zips*	*are, me, the, you*
Quack!, p. 37	**q:** *quack, quick, quit*	*my, the, to, you*
The Pop Quiz, p. 37	**q:** *quick, quiz*	*he, of, she, the, you*

Text Title	Targeted Sound-Spelling or Element	Previously Taught High-Frequency Words
Series 4		
Pat Scans the Ads, p. 38	**s-Blends:** scans, spots, still	like, she, the, two, with
Skipping Snacks, p. 38	**s-Blends:** skip, snack	he, said, to
Bill's Boss, p. 39	**Double Consonants:** boss, staff, tell, yell, yells	he, like
Shake, Rattle, and Buzz, p. 39	**Double Consonants:** bluff, buzz, cliffs, fuss, grass, hiss, off, puff, tell, well, will, yell	do, that, the, to, you
Stan's Quest, p. 40	**Final Blends:** desk, last, pests, quest, rest, task	he, of, that, the, to
A Strong Wind, p. 40	**Final Blends:** brisk, fast, gust, risk	do, of, this, what
Justin's Handheld, p. 41	**Identifying Syllables:** comment, compact, contest, handheld, jacket, pocket	he, this, to
Denim, p. 41	**Identifying Syllables:** denim, fabric, jackets	of, to
Series 5		
Blog Tips, p. 42	**l-Blends:** blab, blog, class, click, glad	for, of, the, to, what, you
Our Camp Blog, p. 42	**l-Blends:** black, blog, bluff, clams, class, plums	for
The Frilly Hat, p. 43	**r-Blends:** brim, frills	he, me, of, the, to, was, what, with
Crazy Cuts, p. 43	**r-Blends:** crop, frizz	me, my, of, you
Cat Tricks, p. 44	**l- and r-Blends:** blanket, tracks	go, her, no, she, the, they
A Big Plan, p. 44	**l- and r-Blends:** plan, plans, truck, trucks, trust	are, do, have, me, said, that, the, to
The Grill is Hot!, p. 45	**Two- and Three-Letter Blends:** black, drop, grab, grill, grim, scrub, splat	from, her, she, that, the, this
Drums Rock!, p. 45	**Two- and Three-Letter Blends:** drum, drumsticks, grabs, grin, plan, strict, strums	he, out, she, the, with, you
Series 6		
The Gift, p. 46	**Final Blends:** craft, expect, gift, help, lamp, left	my, the, to, with, you
Win With Robin's Help, p. 46	**Final Blends:** camp, expect, fact, gift, help, left, stamp, swift	for, have, her, to, we, what, you, your
Frank's Spring Trip, p. 47	**-ng and -nk:** bank, drink, skunk, spring, sting, stinks	from, my, of, the, to, was, with

Summary of Text Elements continued

Text Title	Targeted Sound-Spelling or Element	Previously Taught High-Frequency Words
Series 6 continued		
Art From Junk!, p. 47	**-ng and -nk:** hang, junk, rings, strings	like, of, the
Drastic Measures, p. 48	**Closed Syllables:** basket, drastic, fantastic, hundred, pocket, seven, ticket, traffic	for, he, out, see, the, there, this, to
Fantastic Deals, p. 48	**Closed Syllables:** district, fantastic, picnic, public, subject, sunset, tickets, visit	have, the, to
Grass in the Wind, p. 49	**-nd:** bends, pond, strand, wind	of, to
Fitness Hints, p. 49	**-nt and -nd:** and, bend, blend, bond, hint, send, sprint, stand	by, for, go, of, see, this, to, two, with, you
Series 7		
Trip Snapshots, p. 50	**Digraph sh:** fish, fishing, fresh, shot, snapshot, snapshots, wish	go, me, my, of, that, the, this, to, we
Rush, Josh!, p. 50	**Digraph sh:** finish, rush, shed, shelf, shins	give, no, so, the, to, you
Chimps at Risk, p. 51	**Digraph ch:** chimp, chimps, such	are, be, from, some, that, this, to, was, we
Chuck's Laptop, p. 51	**Digraph ch:** chat, check, chess, much	do, from, he, of, so, the
Catch Some Fun!, p. 52	**-tch:** batch, catch, stretch	for, have, of, or, the
Fetch, Mitch, Fetch!, p. 52	**-tch:** catch, fetch, stretch	do, for, give, he, my, the, to
Dish Trouble, p. 53	**sh, ch, and -tch:** cash, chat, catch, dish, flash, much, rich, shelf, trash	do, for, have, she, the, to, we, with, you
Fresh Water Life, p. 53	**sh and ch:** bunch, fish, fresh, rich, rushes, such	live, of, see, that, what, with, you
Classes For All!, p. 54	**Ending -es:** branches, classes, pitches, sketches, stitches	for, from
Buzz Smashes All Records!, p. 54	**Ending -es:** matches, pitches, smashes, stitches	he, so, to, with, you

Text Title	Targeted Sound-Spelling or Element	Previously Taught High-Frequency Words
Series 8		
Thick Fog Wrecks Ship, p. 55	**Digraph *th*:** them, then, thick, think, this	out, some, the, to, was
Rings and Things, p. 55	**Digraph *th*:** that, them, then, think, this	find, for, go, her, me, new, now, she, the, to, two, you
No Math for Kat, p. 56	**Digraph Review:** broth, chicken, chills, cloth, finish, math, then, this	her, my, of, said, she, you, your
Spelling Champ!, p. 56	**Digraph Review:** champ, matches, math, that, then, think	a, are, he, of, one, said, the, to, you
Cash In on Cleaning Up, p. 57	**Ending *-ing*:** dusting, mopping, picking, polishing, stitching	for, have, like, of, you
Just Checking In, p. 57	**Ending *-ing*:** camping, fishing, resting, sketching, visiting	come, have, he, of, the, was, you
Just What Dad Wanted!, p. 58	**Ending *-ed*:** ended, hinted	could, he, new, or, said, of, what
The Spotted Steps, p. 58	**Ending *-ed*:** planted, sanded, spotted	the, to, was, were
As the Clock Ticked..., p. 59	**Ending *-ed*:** blocked, clapped, dunked, ended, jumped, packed, passed, rushed, ticked, yelled	the, to, were
A Rushed Morning, p. 59	**Ending *-ed*:** dashed, dressed, filled, jumped, missed, mopped, packed, punished, ripped, rushed, spilled	for, my, of, out, the, to, what
Dishing with a Chef, p. 60	**Endings *-ing*, *-ed*:** disgusting, expecting, invented, telling, testing, thrilling, visiting	be, for, here, like, my, no, what, you
Extending Time, p. 60	**Endings *-ing*, *-ed*:** expecting, finishing, getting, missing, yelled	now, the, to, you, your
Series 9		
Desert Mammals, p. 61	**Unstressed Closed Syllables with *a*:** adapt, adapted, affect, constant, mammal, mammals	from, live, of, one, there, they
Instant Fun!, p. 61	**Unstressed Closed Syllables with *a*:** metal, pedal	no, of, out, their, to, you
A Fowl Problem!, p. 62	**Unstressed Closed Syllables with *e*:** chickens, level, problem	have, he, me, of, or, they, to, when, you
Level 10, p. 62	**Unstressed Closed Syllables with *e*:** level, problem, seven, talent	be, could, he, of, one, see, to
Tonsil Trouble, p. 63	**Unstressed Closed Syllables with *i*:** tonsil, tonsils	for, have, me, my, out, said, so, to
A Fossil Fortune?, p. 63	**Unstressed Closed Syllables with *i*:** animal, fossil	for, from, he, my, of, said, was, what

Summary of Text Elements continued

Text Title	Targeted Sound-Spelling or Element	Previously Taught High-Frequency Words
Series 9 continued		
The Grand Canyon, p. 64	**Unstressed Closed Syllables with *o*:** *bottom, canyon, common*	*are, from, of, to*
Trip to the Canyon, p. 64	**Unstressed Closed Syllables with *o*:** *bottom, canyon, common, gallops, seldom*	*are, be, do, from, or, out, they, to, you*
A Helpful Hand, p. 65	**Unstressed Closed Syllables with *u*:** *helpful, thankful, trustful*	*be, good, have, he, me, my, of, out, so, to*
The Cat and the Cactus, p. 65	**Unstressed Closed Syllables with *u*:** *cactus*	*go, my, now, she, to, when*
An Incredible Tale, p. 66	**Consonant + -*le*:** *giggled, impossible, little, prickles, puddle, stumbled, trembled*	*do, have, my, one, was, we, were, what, when, you*
A Little Problem?, p. 66	**Consonant + -*le*:** *crumble, giggled, handle, mumbles, simple, struggle, trembled*	*be, have, he, make, me, my, to, very, we*
Fantastic Travels, p. 67	**Consonant + -*el*, -*al*:** *channel, flannel, nickel, sandals, signaled, travels*	*all, for, me, my, of, some, to, was, what, you, your*
Channel Surfing, p. 67	**Consonant + -*el*, -*al*:** *animal, channel, dental, duffel, jackals, kennel, mammals, medal, pedal, sentimental, travel, travels*	*or, to*

Passage Title	Targeted Sound-Spelling or Element	Previously Taught High-Frequency Words	Glossary Links
Series 10			
The Game, p. 68	**Long a:** base, game plate	for, he, her, their, to, was	home run, pitched
Catch a Wave!, p. 69	**Long a:** hesitate, make, take, takes, tame, wave, waves	are, give, go, have, of, out, to, want, when, you, your	paddle, surfboard
Vines Alive, p. 70	**Long i:** ripe, shine, sides, vine, vines	grow, of, or, to	object, tendril
Free Time, p. 71	**Long i:** bikes, dive, drive, five, kites, like, miles, pine, ride, time, yikes	do, for, from, me, my, to, what, you, your	chill out, rink
Facts About Snakes, p. 72	**Long a, i:** bite, bites, dine, like, name, reptile, scales, slides, snake, snake's, snakes, strikes, wise	are, grow, have, no, or, to, where	prey, venom
The Tale of the Lion and the Fox, p. 73	**Long a, i:** ate, came, cave, smile, time	do, for, me, of, out, said, saw, you, your	suspected, vanished
The Ice Dive, p. 74	**Soft c:** ice, nice, race, raced	do, he, to, two, under, were, you	incredible, record
BMX Bikes Race Fast!, p. 75	**Soft c:** chance, nice, race, races	are, do, down, for, have, of, over, their, they, to, you	crave, strength
The Skywalkers' Challenge, p. 76	**Soft g:** bridge, bridges, challenge, ledge	could, lives, of, over, some, their, they, to, were	constructing, skyscrapers
The Golden Gate Bridge, p. 77	**Soft g:** ages, bridge, cage, edge, gem, magic, stage, strange	from, my, no, of, saw, to, was, what, you	edge of my seat, suspense
A Commitment to Fitness, p. 78	**Suffixes -ment, -ness:** commitment, contentment, fitness, illness, pavement, punishment	do, give, my, of, or, to, we, you, your	commitment, contentment
Run With Quickness, p. 79	**Suffixes -ment, -ness:** commitment, fitness, pavement, punishment	be, do, down, from, keep, these, to, you, your	dashes, sprint
Series 11			
Telling a Good Joke, p. 80	**Long o:** close, hope, joke, jokes, suppose	away, be, do, give, go, my, of, or, say, these, to, too, use, your	chuckle, punch line
The Joke's on You!, p. 81	**Long o:** holes, joked, molehills, moles, ropes	are, because, could, he, my, of, or, out, said, she, some, there, they, what	molehills, nibble
A Huge (and Fun) Job, p. 82	**Long u:** amusing, confuse, cute, excuses, huge, use	are, have, of, or, so, the, when, you, your	instill, kibble

Summary of Text Elements continued

Passage Title	Targeted Sound-Spelling or Element	Previously Taught High-Frequency Words	Glossary Links
Series 11 continued			
A Tribute to Amelia Bloomer, p. 83	**Long u:** *amused, disputed, fumed, tribute*	*could, lives, of, she, so, these, to, was*	*corset, tribute*
Ruthless Reptile!, p. 84	**VCe Syllables:** *despite, escape, lunchtime, mistake, reptile, reptile's*	*be, for, of, or, to, too, under, very, when*	*temperature, unsuspecting*
Contribute Now!, p. 85	**VCe Syllables:** *classmates, compute, contribute, invite, lemonade, trombones*	*about, are, be, doing, for, some, they, to, we, your*	*compute, contribute*
Letters to *The Tribune*, p. 86	**VCe Syllables:** *advice, dispute, inflated, mistake, mistaken, online, oppose, price, statements, those*	*about, are, my, of, see, their, to, who*	*pay the price, shrubs*
A Bug to Admire, p. 87	**VCe Syllables:** *entire, inside, mistake*	*are, do, does, down, for, he, keep, of, she, so, they, to*	*fungus, predators*
Lunch Nonsense, p. 88	**Prefixes *un-, non-, de-:*** *deflated, defrost, nonsense, nonstick, nonstop, unripe*	*all, are, be, for, go, good, me, my, of, out, say, she, they, to, was, we, were*	*ripe, stressed me out*
A Nonstop Process, p. 89	**Prefixes *un-, non-, de-:*** *decompose, decomposed, nonstop, uninvited*	*be, because, go, grow, live, of, these, they, to, we, when*	*organisms, process*
Series 12			
Gliding in Thin Air, p. 90	**Ending *-ing* (drop e):** *changing, exciting, gliding*	*down, from, or, to, you, your*	*imagine, prone*
Trading Places, p. 91	**Ending *-ing* (drop e):** *biking, diving, frustrating, gliding, hiking, skating, trading, wading*	*all, from, have, he, me, my, said, to, what, you, your*	*hang gliding, wading*
Scrubbing Jake, p. 92	**Ending *-ing* (with doubling):** *dragging, getting, jogging, kidding, quitting, stopping, swimming, winning*	*does, give, he, me, my, no, of, one, said, to, was, what, when*	*in a flash, resist*
Pinch Hitting, p. 93	**Ending *-ing* (with doubling):** *admitting, batting, gripping, jogging, kidding, scanning, stepping, quitting*	*could, good, he, into, of, over, saw, their, to, two, was, who*	*sidelines, teammates*
Visited by Ms. Rush, p. 94	**Ending *-ed* (drop e):** *joked, liked, smiled, voted, waved*	*about, be, because, for, have, her, said, she, to, was, when*	*candidate, environment*
Puzzled by Nature?, p. 95	**Ending *-ed* (drop e):** *chuckled, dozed, gazed, puzzled, smiled*	*all, grow, growing, have, he, me, my, no, of, said, saw, to, under, when, who*	*dozed, unwise*

Passage Title	Targeted Sound-Spelling or Element	Previously Taught High-Frequency Words	Glossary Links
Series 12 continued			
A Badly Planned Surprise, p. 96	**Ending -ed (with doubling):** *crammed, grabbed, stepped, stopped*	*be, for, have, looks, me, no, of, said, she, to, was, what*	*supposed, surprise*
I Visited L.A.!, p. 97	**Ending -ed (with doubling):** *dropped, drummed, flipped, hopped, shopped, sipped, strummed*	*by, of, out, saw, some, they, to, was, we, who*	*boardwalk, juggled*
Series 13			
Spy Nancy Wake, p. 98	**y:** *spy, try*	*could, for, her, of, one, she, they, to, was*	*smuggled, radio codes*
This Guy Can Fly!, p. 99	**y:** *dry, fly, flying, shy, skydived, try, trying*	*are, away, for, from, he, of, only, see, to, we*	*deserts, microlight plane*
Is Cricket Trendy?, p. 100	**y:** *city, copy, happy, lucky, trendy, tricky*	*are, for, from, he, look, now, of, or, out, they, to, was, would, you, your*	*comeback, immigrants*
A Risky Trip, p. 101	**y:** *angry, chilly, dizzy, hungry, ninety, plenty, rocky, safety, silly*	*are, be, come, do, for, from, go, have, her, me, of, said, so, their, to, was, we, you*	*compass, steep*
A Clever Gym Plan, p. 102	**y:** *gym, gym's, system*	*about, be, do, have, how, me, of, out, to, too, you*	*classical, system*
Cyndy's Email, p. 103	**y:** *cymbals, gym, gymnastics*	*be, from, have, me, no, of, said, their, to, we, would, you*	*cymbals, offense*
Lucky to Be Alive!, p. 104	**Suffixes -y, -ly:** *chilly, frosty, lucky, quickly, rapidly, risky, sadly, safely*	*be, from, of, they, to, two, was, were, who*	*snowshoes, survivors*
Slimy Slugs, p. 105	**Suffixes -y, -ly:** *quickly, slimy, snugly, sticky*	*are, for, many, one, or, see, to, what, you*	*tentacles, tunnels*
Amazing Mummies, p.106	**Changing -y to -i:** *bodies, dried, enemies, luckily, mummies, spied*	*about, for, from, have, he, of, out, over, their, to, was, what, when*	*decompose, organs*
Nadia Flies!, p. 107	**Changing -y to -i:** *dummies, luckily, skies, supplied, tried*	*be, because, do, for, from, her, lived, of, or, she, they, to, was*	*special effects, stunts*
Whale Spotting, p. 108	**wh:** *whale, whales, when, whips*	*all, are, come, down, for, from, have, look, of, out, some, they, to, you*	*mammals, migrate*
Alexandra Courtis Is a Whiz, p. 109	**wh:** *while, whiz*	*could, from, have, her, of, she, to, was, were*	*cancer, process*
Elephants, p.110	**ph:** *elephant, elephants*	*are, because, for, how, of, so, these, to, where*	*energy, liquid*
Cell Phone, Please, p. 111	**ph:** *phone, phones, phrases, phony*	*about, are, be, call, could, do, from, have, no, of, or, they, to, we, what, you, your*	*fad, in a jam*

Summary of Text Elements continued

Passage Title	Targeted Sound-Spelling or Element	Previously Taught High-Frequency Words	Glossary Links
Series 14			
What's Wrong?, p. 112	**Silent Consonants:** *knock, knocking, wreck, wrong*	*about, are, me, to, want*	*adjusting, off-key*
Finding a Shipwreck, p. 113	**Silent Consonants:** *knock, shipwrecks, wreck, written, wrong*	*about, all, be, go, or, some, they, to, too*	*gems, treasures*
A Cable Crisis, p. 114	**Open Syllables:** *bacon, cable, even, relax, table, vacant*	*are, call, down, for, no, of, so, to, too, was*	*plopped, vacant*
The Dependable Truck, p. 115	**Open Syllables:** *cable, depends, frequently, legal, table, vacant, vehicle, vehicles*	*are, away, have, many, of, or, out, their, there, to, you, your*	*fines, wreck*
A Bonobo Named Kanzi, p. 116	**Open Syllables:** *Bonobo, Bonobos, Congo, humans, even, microwave, open, program, unit*	*are, for, from, how, live, lives, of, one, they, to*	*vending machine, vocabulary*
Secrets of America's Big Cat, p. 117	**Open Syllables:** *defense, distributed, humans, humid, menu, moment, Yukon*	*are, come, do, from, live, many, never, these, they, to, you, your*	*confront, defense*
An Amazing Animal, p. 118	**Unstressed Open Syllables:** *along, amazing, animal, habitat, identify, tentacles*	*about, down, for, have, look, looks, of, they, to, want*	*nerves, striking*
A Complicated Insect, p. 119	**Unstressed Open Syllables:** *adults, amazing, celebrated, complicated, colonies, colony, define, divided, habitat, magnificent, represent, selected*	*about, all, because, do, have, into, more, most, of, some, to, you*	*inhabit, system*
The Six Hills Shopping Complex, p. 120	**Prefixes *con-, com-:** combines, committed, complex, confess, confidence, connect, connected, contact, continent*	*any, are, every, for, from, have, new, of, or, to, where, you, your*	*complex, confidence*
Committed to Change, p. 121	**Prefixes *con-, com-:** combine, commented, committed, confess, conflicted, construct, contemplate*	*are, does, from, give, look, looks, of, said, some, these, they, to, who, you, your*	*contemplate, envy*
Series 15			
Training Rocky, p. 122	***ai:** exclaimed, plain, tail, train, trained, training, trains*	*every, give, good, now, or, over, said, to, was, you*	*commanded, gobbled*
A Painted History, p. 123	***ai:** details, jail, nail, nails, painted, painting, stained, stains*	*about, are, could, for, have, of, or, some, their, these, was, who, you, your*	*status, tints*
A Snow Day in Dubai, p. 124	***ay:** day, days, may, midday, play, stray*	*first, here, look, of, some, soon, to, you, your*	*artificial, Middle East*

Passage Title	Targeted Sound-Spelling or Element	Previously Taught High-Frequency Words	Glossary Links
Series 15 continued			
Stay in Shape, p. 125	**ay:** *away, daytime, pay, play, stay, way*	*do, from, good, of, or, these, to, you, your*	*in a rut, traffic*
Why Can't She Explain?, p. 126	**Long *a* Vowel Team Syllables:** *complain, explain, maintain, plain, rain, say, stay, Sunday, way*	*any, are, one, or, there, to, you*	*in a huff, made it plain*
The Laptop Complaint, p. 127	**Long *a* Vowel Team Syllables:** *complain, complained, day, days, detail, explained, okay, pay, say*	*for, from, have, new, of, one, or, they, to, what, you, your*	*company, manufacturer*
Series 16			
What Makes Soap Float?, p. 128	**oa:** *coat, float, soap, soaps*	*for, how, of, some, they, to, what*	*density, liquid*
Callahan's Boat, p. 129	**oa:** *afloat, boat, floating*	*could, give, good, have, into, of, to, was*	*capsized, spear*
A City Garden Grows, p. 130	**ow:** *flow, grow, growth, own, show, snows, windows*	*about, are, how, many, of, pretty, their, they, to, what*	*greenhouse, system*
Do You Know Stan Lee?, p. 131	**ow:** *grow, know, known, row, showed*	*all, are, been, could, have, many, of, see, to, too, were, you*	*admired, characters*
Who Owns the Roads?, p. 132	**Long *o* Vowel Team Syllables:** *approached, blowing, followed, load, own, road, roads, roadway, roadways, thrown*	*all, could, do, every, now, of, one, there, to, too, was, what*	*adopt, dodge*
Danger on the Coast, p. 133	**Long *o* Vowel Team Syllables:** *coast, coastline, coated, goal, know, knowing, mowed, yellow*	*any, are, come, from, into, of, their, they, to, was, were, who*	*eliminate, thrived*
Series 17			
An Idea to Rethink, p. 134	**Prefixes *re-*, *pre-*:** *prepaid, preteen, refill, rethink*	*could, for, have, into, of, put, said, to, want, was, what, would, you*	*broke, shot*
The Rewriter's Life, p. 135	**Prefixes *re-*, *pre-*:** *prewriting, recheck, rewriting*	*about, all, always, are, do, have, her, how, lives, of, said, to, want, was, you, your*	*novelist, research*
Reaching His Goal, p. 136	**ea:** *beat, bleak, dream, each, reached, reading, speaking, team, teams*	*about, could, their, these, they, was, who*	*bleak, evidence*
Beach Clean-Up Day, p. 137	**ea:** *beach, clean, each, jeans, least, sea, seashell, teams*	*all, do, for, looked, of, one, or, to, two, was, were*	*crumpled, volunteers*
The Lighthouse Keeper, p. 138	**ee:** *deep, fleets, keep, teeth*	*for, of, out, there, they, to, was, who, would*	*fleets, lighthouse*

Summary of Text Elements continued

Passage Title	Targeted Sound-Spelling or Element	Previously Taught High-Frequency Words	Glossary Links
Series 17 continued			
Deep, Deep Quicksand, p. 139	*ee: creepy, deep, feet, knees, seen*	*do, of, soon, to, under, what, you*	*thrashing, vanish*
A Niece's Mistake, p. 140	*ie: believe, chief, field, niece, retrieves*	*before, for, have, her, there, to, who, your*	*niece, precinct*
The Chiefs and the Bobcats, p. 141	*ie: brief, chiefs, field, shrieked, yielded*	*first, for, from, how, never, they, to, was, were, you*	*blocked, yielded*
America's Bald Eagles, p. 142	**Long e Vowel Team Syllables:** *between, eagles, decrease, decreased, fields, leaked, streams, weak*	*have, into, live, there, these, to, was, were*	*absorbed, tainted*
Sleepy Teens!, p. 143	**Long e Vowel Team Syllables:** *asleep, feel, ideal, keep, least, need, reason, sleep, teen, teens, weekdays, weekends*	*about, after, are, before, for, have, of, these, they, to, who, you*	*concentrate, schedule*
Series 18			
Insight Into a Dog's Mind, p. 144	*igh: bright, frightened, high, might, slightly*	*are, for, how, look, or, out, they, you*	*predict, snarls*
A Mighty Runner, p. 145	*igh: delight, sight, slightly*	*after, again, around, could, first, for, never, or, would*	*depression, stroke*
A Wild Feast, p. 146	**Other Long Vowel Spellings:** *bold, kind, kinds, mind, wild*	*before, do, does, down, give, of, once, one, to, was, what, you*	*anesthetic, champion*
Taking Tolls (and Loving It!), p. 147	**Other Long Vowel Spellings:** *cold, find, jolts, kind, mind, told, toll, tolls*	*about, after, all, for, have, how, looks, many, now, of, one, said, to, was, what, work*	*attitude, jolts*
An Uncomplicated Request, p. 148	**Analyzing Word Structure:** *uncomplicated, unluckily*	*before, for, from, have, her, of, or, you*	*colonists, pirates*
Is Cave Life Unappealing?, p. 149	**Analyzing Word Structure:** *decomposing, unappealing, uncomplicated, unlimited*	*are, do, for, have, never, of, some, their, these, they, to*	*remains, senses*

Passage Title	Targeted Sound-Spelling or Element	Previously Taught High-Frequency Words	Glossary Links
Series 19			
Smart Sharks, p. 150	*ar:* large, part, sharks, smart	again, are, do, for, of, some, their, they, to, would, you	experimenting, scientists
Stars in the Sky, p. 151	*ar:* dark, far, star, starlight, stars, yard	are, because, live, looked, of, said, their, to, your	constellation, satellite
Artist Diego Rivera, p. 152	**Syllables with *ar:*** alarming, art, artist, artists, charcoal, large, part, regarded, start	about, because, for, of, one, was	political, society
A Startling Find, p. 153	**Syllables with *ar:*** discarded, March, parchment, smart, yard	about, because, been, for, goes, how, of, one, out, said, some, to, what, who	parchment, treasure
Within Her Reach!, p. 154	*er:* after, government, her, modern, nerves, offered, over, person's, serving	about, are, because, do, for, have, now, of, or, there, these, to, together, was, who, would	limbs, technology
Making a Difference, p. 155	*er:* better, difference, elderly, emergency, herself, members, offer, person, shelters, serve, terrific	about, all, are, do, have, of, or, there, to, would, you, your	elderly, volunteer
A Bird Puzzle, p. 156	*ir:* birch, bird, birds, chirping, confirm, dirt, stirring, squirming, twirl	about, are, been, every, how, of, out, they, to	cradle, soothe
Bird Talk, p. 157	*ir:* bird, birds	any, does, for, give, have, of, one, or, said, these, to, together, two, want, what, where, who, you	not to be taken seriously, sayings
Safe Web Surfing Tips, p. 158	*ur:* curb, disturbs, hurt, surf, surfing, surprisingly, turn, turns	are, give, into, of, says, some, someone, you, your	curb, hacked
Surfing the Pavement, p. 159	*ur:* curve, curves, surfboard, surfing, turns	around, been, down, for, have, how, look, of, or, out, these, to	made a splash, stable
Attack of the Spiders!, p. 160	**Syllables with *er, ir, ur:*** computer, computers, concerned, furry, girl, her, letters, other, printer, spider, spiders, squirming, surprised, terminal	are, do, have, of, out, said, some, their, these, they, to, two, was, what, would, you	keyboard, tarantula
Thirsty? Drink Up!, p. 161	**Syllables with *er, ir, ur:*** after, danger, during, exercise, intervals, percent, person's, summer, thirsty, whether	about, before, of, or, they, to, you, your	cramps, pulse
Glaciers in Greenland, p. 162	*ci:* glacier, self-sufficient, social	also, become, been, for, four, have, many, one, to, their, they	Arctic Circle, self-sufficient
The Special Olympics, p. 163	*ci:* officials, special	come, could, do, from, good, new, now, of, one, there, they, to, too, two, want, was	disability, foundation

Summary of Text Elements continued

Passage Title	Targeted Sound-Spelling or Element	Previously Taught High-Frequency Words	Glossary Links
Series 19 continued			
Dr. Fraction's Contraptions, p. 164	*ti:* attention, contraption, invention, inventions, motion	all, always, are, been, before, for, from, many, new, now, of, one, pretty, said, they, to, was, you, your	contraption, inventions
Motion Sickness in Space, p. 165	*ti:* attention, conditions, direction, motion, notion, position	are, around, down, from, have, of, or, they, to, what	gravity, nausea
Series 20			
A Model Sailor, p. 166	**or:** cords, sort, sport, sportsmanship	could, have, of, out, said, to, was, were, who, would	capsized, postponed
A Tornado Ride, p. 167	**or:** north, shorts, sport, storm, tornado	all, good, of, out, to, was	roared, tornado
Funnel-Web Spiders, p. 168	**ore:** before, explore, ignore, more	any, do, does, live, of, their, these, they, to, you	explore, extremely
Gold on the Seashore p. 169	**ore:** before, explore, explored, ignore, more, ore, seashore, shore, wore	could, do, down, of, one, out, there, they, to, was, you	miners, ore
Weather Reports, p. 170	**Syllables with or, ore:** categories, corner, for, forecast, important, information, ignore, or, organized, report, stormy	every, of, out, to, you, your	forecast, local
A Memorable Performance, p. 171	**Syllables with or, ore:** before, corner, for, glory, important, morning, performed, record, sort, wore	always, down, give, good, have, how, now, of, saw, to, was, would, you	career, chills down her spine
Andrew Clements, Writer, p. 172	**Suffixes -er, -or:** editor, manager, songwriter, teacher, writer	have, how, many, now, of, one, to, was, you	managed, publishing
Former Track Star Becomes Swimmer, p. 173	**Suffixes -er, -or:** beginner, instructor, joker, reporter, runner, swimmer, teacher	are, does, from, give, good, have, new, of, out, put, said, to, too, was, would, you, your	athletic, track
The Three Bears, p. 174	**Suffixes -er, -est:** brightest, chillier, chilliest, cleaner, cleanest, darker, darkest, faster, highest, happier	could, have, here, of, one, their, they, together, was, you	complaining, moonlight
Which Pole Is Coldest?, p. 175	**Suffixes -er, -est:** colder, coldest, drier, higher, highest	are, from, have, of, out, they	elevation, station

Passage Title	Targeted Sound-Spelling or Element	Previously Taught High-Frequency Words	Glossary Links
Series 20 continued			
That Is Some Haircut!, p. 176	*air*: airplanes, chairs, haircut, pair, repairing, upstairs, wheelchairs	all, come, from, new, of, put, they, to, two	bells and whistles, feel like a million bucks
The Story of the Chair, p. 177	*air*: chair, chairs, pairs	are, come, do, from, now, of, one, to, was	ancient, century
A Giant Hare, p. 178	*are*: care, compared, hare, hares, shared, stare	of, said, they	breed, hare
A Very Rare Bat, p. 179	*are*: compare, rare, spare, square, stare, welfare	about, are, because, do, have, live, many, of, one, their, there, these, they, to, was, what	fate, welfare
A Pair of Pears for Mr. Hill, p. 180	*ear*: pears, wear	always, around, laugh, now, of, one, out, pretty, some, their, to, was, would, you, your	corny, spare
Where Did Bear Go?, p. 181	*ear*: swear, tear, wearing	are, around, been, do, give, new, of, one, out, put, saw, their, they, to, want, was, were, what, where, would	flyers, updated
Grasshopper Nightmare, p. 182	Syllables with *air, are, ear*: despair, prepared, scare, scared, shared, wearing	about, are, been, many, new, of, one, their, they, to, too, was	bonnet, hardships
Cancer Scare, p. 183	Syllables with *air, are, ear*: aware, careful, careless, repair, scary, share, sharing, wearing	always, are, could, four, from, of, one, they, to, two, was, who	beamed, scarring
Series 21			
Gold Coin Mine, p. 184	*oi*: choice, coin, joined, soil	their, they, to, two, was, were	construct, profit
A Car With a Voice, p. 185	*oi*: avoid, choice, noise, pointers, spoils, voice	because, from, have, many, of, some, their, these, they, to, want, who, would, you, your	devices, digital
Soy Milk, p. 186	*oy*: soy, soybeans	are, do, from, many, of, one, some, their, these, to, was, you, your	filtered, healthy
Toy Time, p. 187	*oy*: boy, enjoy, joy, toy, toys	about, all, any, are, from, how, new, of, out, they, to	construction, equipment
From Disappointment to Rejoicing, p. 188	Syllables with *oi, oy*: annoyed, destroy, disappointing, rejoice	all, could, do, how, of, put, soon, these, they, to, was, were, what, work	co-worker, flop
Are Messes Annoying or Helpful?, p. 189	Syllables with *oi, oy*: annoyance, avoid, point, voicing	are, because, some, together, were, you, your	creativity, penicillin

Summary of Text Elements continued

Passage Title	Targeted Sound-Spelling or Element	Previously Taught High-Frequency Words	Glossary Links
Series 21 continued			
A City Rebounds, p. 190	*ou*: about, amounts, cloudless, countless, mouth, proud, rebounding, South, thousands, without	because, many, new, of, to, was, were	levees, surge
Party Countdown, p. 191	*ou*: cloud, count, ground, loud, pound, proud, sounds, south, thousands	many, new, of, some, they, to	celebration, tradition
Too Small to Prowl, p. 192	*ow*: brown, down, downstairs, frowned, growling, how, howling, meow, now, prowling, scowling, towel	all, are, of, said, to, too, was, what, you	prowling, scowling
Clowning and Krumping, p. 193	*ow*: bow, clown, clowning, crowds, how, renowned, south, wow	are, do, look, of, some, their, these, they, to, two	coordination, evolving
An Astounding Work of Art, p. 194	**Syllables with *ou*, *ow*:** allowed, astounding, background, downtown, found, nowadays, renowned	any, many, new, some, to, what, where, work, you	ceiling, Sistine Chapel
Powerful Listening Skills, p. 195	**Syllables with *ou*, *ow*:** aloud, amount, announces, drowsy	good, of, these, to, what, you, your	concentrate, opinions
Series 22			
Sleepless in a Science Experiment, p.196	**Suffixes -*less*, -*ful*:** grateful, helpful, sleepless, useful	of, to, two, was	science fair, specialist
Fearless Badger, p. 197	**Suffixes -*less*, -*ful*:** defenseless, fearless, powerful, useful	any, are, because, do, of, one, their, these, they, to, want, you	carnivorous, larvae
Old Noodles, p. 198	*oo*: food, mood, noodles, proof	all, are, from, good, have, pretty, they, to, was, were, what, who, you, your	archeologists, earthquake
Space Boots, p. 199	*oo*: boots, cool, moon	from, have, many, of, one, these, they, to, walk, were, what, who, you	astronauts, fashionable
Blackbeard in the News, p.200	*ew*: crew, news	of, one, their, there, to, was, were	cargo, merchant
News About Bigfoot, p. 201	*ew*: drew, news, slew	are, because, does, many, their, they, to, what	flimsy, hoaxes
The Musical Flute, p. 202	*u_e*: crude, flute, flutes, flutist, flutist's, include, included, includes, tube, tune, tunes	are, does, from, many, of, some, to, were, you	mammoths, reed
Singing Sand Dunes, p. 203	*u_e*: dune, dunes, produced	are, do, of, said, these, you	clash, majestic

Passage Title	Targeted Sound-Spelling or Element	Previously Taught High-Frequency Words	Glossary Links
Series 22 continued			
A Jewel in Space, p. 204	**Syllables with oo, ew, u_e:** crudely, including, jewel, knew, moon	do, from, looked, looking, of, said, these, they, to, today, was, were, you	atmosphere, international
Renew Your Look, p. 205	**Syllables with oo, ew, u_e:** attitude, cool, costume jewelry, hoopskirts, loosened, new, newspaper, poodle, renew	always, are, come, do, everyone, have, of, one, some, there, these, to, want, who, you, your	trendy, unique
Series 23			
Jake Farriss Gets Cooking, p. 206	**oo:** book, cookbook, cooking, look	anyone, could, friends, of, one, their, they, to, were, who, would, you	impressed, recipes
Handmade Books, p. 207	**oo:** book, books, took, wooden	called, could, of, to, together, was	designs, scribe
Stop Pulling My Leg!, p. 208	**u:** bull, full, pulled, push	do, from, some, to, what	block, phrase
Pushing the Limits, p. 209	**u:** bush, fully, pulled, push, pushed	are, been, come, every, everything, of, one, there, two	clenched, series
Cook, the Ten-Foot Rookie, p. 210	**Syllables with oo, u:** foot, fulfill, good, hoof, looking, outlook, push, rookie	are, do, from, of, one, their, to	honor, rookie
Wooden Shoes, p. 211	**Syllables with oo, u:** cushy, footsteps, footwear, looking, pushing, wood, wooden	all, are, been, from, of, some, their, they, to, walk, were, would, you, your	cushy, Netherlands
It's the Law, p. 212	**aw:** drawn, law, lawn, laws	are, four, from, have, many, of, some, these, to, was, were, you, your	illegal, outdated
All About Straw, p. 213	**aw:** straw	been, from, have, of, some, their, there, to, what	harvested, recycled
Author and Baseball Fan, p. 214	**au:** applaud, author, haunting, launched	are, have, many, of, to, what, who	passion, sinister
Launching Into Flight, p. 215	**au:** applauded, launch, launching, precautions, taunted	are, do, from, have, into, many, of, they, to, would, you	harness, precautions
Crazy Rainfall, p. 216	**a:** all, chalk, fallen, rainfall, small	from, have, of, one, there, these, they, thought, very, water, were, what, words	meteors, theory
Don't Call a Wasp a Bee!, p. 217	**a:** call, fallen, walls, wasp	are, both, build, live, they, two, you	pollen, segments
A Flawless Player, p. 218	**Syllables with aw, au, a:** all, always, audition, baseball, baseball's, law, taunted	could, enough, to, was	color line, excelled
Watch, Read, and Applaud, p. 219	**Syllables with aw, au, a:** also, always, applaud, awfully, automatically, because, called, falling, yawns	are, do, language, most, of, sometimes, there, to, you	automatically, foreign

Summary of Text Elements continued

Passage Title	Targeted Sound-Spelling or Element	Previously Taught High-Frequency Words	Glossary Links
Series 24			
Subways Move Us, p. 220	**Prefixes *mid-, sub-*:** midday, midtown, suburbs, subway, subways	from, have, of, one, these, they, to, you	midtown, transportation
Three Pigs in the Suburbs, p. 221	**Prefixes *mid-, sub-*:** midnight, midsized, midtown, sublet, suburbs, subway	again, buy, could, of, one, to, was, where	plunked down, sublet
A Tasty Mistake, p. 222	**Prefixes *dis-, mis-*:** disagreed, disliked, misjudged, mistake	goes, loved, of, one, these, to, too, was, would	picky, soggy
A Disappearing Dog Leads to Discovery, p. 223	**Prefixes *dis-, mis-*:** disappeared, dismayed, misbehaving, miscalculation, misjudged, mistreated	are, could, from, have, of, to, was	dismayed, hesitant
Sports and Smoking: A Losing Combination, p. 224	**Suffixes *-tion, -sion*:** circulation, combination, decision, explanation	are, do, from, of, they, to, who	addictive, oxygen
Let the Celebrations Begin!, p. 225	**Suffixes *-tion, -sion*:** celebrations, collection, competition, decision, decorations, imaginations, vacation	from, here, of, these, to, where, you, your	concrete, Luxembourg
America's Incredible Teen Inventor, p. 226	**Suffixes *-able, -ible*:** believable, recognizable, responsible, valuable	could, do, of, one, their, there, to, two, was, work, you	royalties, transmitted
Simply Unbelievable!, p. 227	**Suffixes *-able, -ible*:** edible, memorable, reasonable, sensible, unbelievable, unforgettable	any, are, could, do, from, have, into, of, their, these, they, thought, to, what, you, your	edible, gadgets
History of the Bicycle, p. 228	**Prefixes *uni-, bi-, tri-*:** bicycle, bicycles, tricycle, unicycle	most, of, one, to, today, there, two, was, you	terrain, vehicle
Thrilling Triathlons, p. 229	**Prefixes *uni-, bi-, tri-*:** bicycle, triathlete, triathletes, triathlon, triathlons, triple, uniform	are, every, of, one, some, they, to, who	brutal, excel

Passage Title	Targeted Sound-Spelling or Element	Previously Taught High-Frequency Words	Glossary Links
Series 25			
Autograph or Autopen?, p. 230	**Roots *bio, graph, auto*:** autograph, autographs, automatically, autopen, photograph	*again, been, does, have, of, one, there, to, two, you*	*automatically, handwritten*
Autobiographies and Biographies, p. 231	**Roots *bio, graph, auto*:** autobiography, biographies, biography, photographs, photography	*been, from, have, of, one, these, they, what, who, you, your*	*likeness, subject*
Cuban Import Goes Bananas!, p. 232	**Roots *port, dict*:** imported, predicted, seaport	*are, could, from, have, of, one, they, to, was, were, what*	*produce, pushcarts*
Important Figures in Fashion, p. 233	**Roots *port, dict*:** important, imported, predicted, reports, seaport	*are, could, from, of, they, was, work*	*immigrant, rivets*
Mt. St. Helens Erupts!, p. 234	**Roots *rupt, struct, scrib/script*:** destruction, erupt, erupted, eruption, instructions, prescribe	*again, any, from, of, they*	*avalanche, crater*
Deadly Destruction, p. 235	**Roots *rupt, struct, scrib/script*:** constructed, descriptions, destruction	*of, some, they, was, were, where, would*	*disasters, outbreak*
An Invisible Force, p. 236	**Roots *scope, tele, phon, vis/vid*:** evidence, invisible, telescope	*are, from, of, their, they, to, together, your*	*astronomers, galaxies*
A Saxophonist Supreme, p. 237	**Roots *scope, tele, phon, vis/vid*:** saxophone, saxophonist, video	*of, one, they, to, what*	*composer, critics*

Glossary

▶ A glossary is a useful tool found at the back of many books. It contains useful information about key words in the texts.

ab•sorb
(ab-**zorb**) *verb*
To soak up liquid. *The sponge will absorb the juice.*

ad•dic•tive
(uh-**dik**-tive) *adjective*
Very hard to give it up. *Smoking is addictive.*

ad•just
(uh-**juhst**) *verb*
1. To move or change something slightly. *Evan needs to adjust the picture on the wall.*
2. To get used to something new and different. *Jenny will adjust to living in a new city.*

ad•mire
(ad-**mire**) *verb*
To like and respect. *I admire my math teacher because she is very patient.*

a•dopt
(uh-**dopt**) *verb*
To choose to take care of someone or something, such as when adults take a child into their family and become his or her legal parents. *The family will adopt a baby.*

an•cient
(**ayn**-shunt) *adjective*
Belonging to a time long ago. *The museum had several statues from ancient Rome.*

an•es•thet•ic
(an-iss-**thet**-ik) *noun*
A drug or a gas given to people before an operation so that they do not feel pain. *The dentist gave Dave an anesthetic before pulling his tooth.*

ar•chae•o•lo•gist
(ar-kee-**ol**-uh-jist) *noun*
Someone who studies the past by digging up old buildings and objects and examining them carefully. *The archaeologist discovered many dinosaur bones.*

archaeologist

Arc•tic Cir•cle
(**ark**-tik **sur**-kuhl) *noun*
An imaginary line that runs through the northern parts of Canada, Alaska, Russia, and Scandinavia at 66 ½ degrees north latitude. *The Arctic Circle marks the area where the sun never sets on the longest day of the year.*

art•i•fi•cial
(ar-ti-**fish**-uhl) *adjective*
False, not real. *I'm surprised that the flowers are artificial, and not real.*

as•tro•naut
(**as**-truh-nawt) *noun*
Someone who travels in space. *The astronaut flew the spaceship to the moon.*

as•tron•o•mer
(uh-**stron**-uh-mur) *noun*
Someone who studies the stars, planets, and space. *The astronomer discovered a new star.*

ath•let•ic
(ath-**let**-ik) *adjective*
To be very good at sports or games that require speed, strength, or skill. *Tracy was always athletic and liked playing sports.*

at•mos•phere
(**at**-muhss-fihr) *noun*
The mixture of gases that surrounds a planet. *The spaceship traveled through all the layers of Earth's atmosphere when returning from space.*

at•ti•tude
(**at**-i-tood) *noun*
A person's opinions or feelings about someone or something. *Theo has a positive attitude toward his work.*

au•to•mat•i•cal•ly
(aw-tuh-**mat**-ik-uh-lee) *adverb*
Happening on its own or without an operator. *The timer rings automatically once an hour.*

av•a•lanche
(**av**-uh-lanch) *noun*
A large amount of snow, ice, or earth that suddenly moves down the side of a mountain. *The skiers got caught in an avalanche.*

beam
(**beem**)
1. *verb*
To smile widely. *Seeing the "A" on his report made Greg beam.*
2. *noun*
A ray or band of light. *The flashlight beam lit up the path.*

beam

> **bells and whistles**
> (**belz and wiss**-uhlz) *idiom*
> Additional features or extras. *His new car comes with all the bells and whistles, like leather seats and a sunroof.*

bleak
(**bleek**) *adjective*
Without hope. *The prisoner's life was bleak.*

block
(**blok**)
1. *verb*
To stop something from getting past. *The basketball player jumped to block the shot.*
2. *noun*
The area from one street to another. *Sid lives only one block away from his school.*

board•walk
(**bord**-wawk) *noun*
A wooden walkway along a beach or waterfront. *We sat on the boardwalk and watched the ships sail in.*

bon•net
(**bon**-it) *noun*
A baby's or woman's hat, tied with strings under the chin. *The bonnet shaded the baby's face from the sun.*

breed
(**breed**) *noun*
A particular type of animal. *A pug is a breed of dog.*

broke
(**brohk**) *adjective*
To have no money. *Ted was broke after he spent his allowance on games.*

Glossary continued

bru•tal
(**broo**-tuhl) *adjective*
Harsh and severe. *The last mile of the marathon was brutal.*

can•cer
(**kan**-sur) *noun*
A serious disease in which some cells in the body grow faster than normal cells and destroy healthy organs and tissues. *Cyclist Lance Armstrong is a cancer survivor.*

can•di•date
(**kan**-duh-date) *noun*
Someone who is applying for a job or running in an election. *Jim's aunt is a candidate for mayor.*

cap•size
(**kap**-size) *verb*
To turn over in the water. *A large wave can cause a boat to capsize.*

ca•reer
(kuh-**rihr**) *noun*
The work or the series of jobs that a person has over time. *The actress has a successful film career.*

car•go
(**kar**-goh) *noun*
The goods that are carried by a ship, plane, truck, or other type of transportation. *The dock workers unloaded the ship's cargo at the port.*

cargo

car•niv•o•rous
(kar-**niv**-ur-uhss) *adjective*
Meat-eating. *Wolves are carnivorous animals that eat smaller animals, such as rodents and rabbits.*

ceil•ing
(**see**-ling) *noun*
The upper surface inside a room. *She painted her bedroom ceiling with stars, so she could look up at them at night.*

cel•e•bra•tion
(sel-uh-**bray**-shuhn) *noun*
A joyous ceremony or gathering, usually to mark a major event. *There was a huge celebration on the last day of school.*

cen•tu•ry
(**sen**-chuh-ree) *noun*
A period of 100 years. *Their house was built over a century ago.*

cham•pi•on
(**cham**-pee-uhn) *noun*
The winner of a competition or tournament. *Zoë was the state champion in skateboarding this year.*

char•ac•ter
(**ka**-rik-tur) *noun*
A person in a story, book, play, movie, or television program. *Captain Hook is a character in Peter Pan.*

chill out
(**chil** out) *phrasal verb*
To relax. *After a long day at school, Carrie likes to chill out by listening to music.*

chuck•le
(**chuh**-kuhl) *noun*
A quiet laugh. *I had a good chuckle when he told me the joke.*

clash
(**klash**) *noun*
A loud, crashing sound. *We heard the clash of cymbals.*

clas•si•cal
(**klass**-uh-kuhl) *adjective*
1. Music that is timeless, serious, and in the European tradition, such as opera, chamber music, and symphony. *We went to a classical music concert featuring one of Beethoven's symphonies.*
2. In the style of ancient Greece or Rome. *The design of the courthouse was based on classical architecture.*

clench
(**klench**) *verb*
To hold or squeeze something tightly. *Maria would clench her fists when she was angry.*

col•o•nist
(**kol**-uh-nist) *noun*
Someone who lives in a newly settled area. *Peter Minuit was a Dutch colonist who bought Manhattan from the Native Americans.*

color line
(**kuhl**-ur **line**) *noun*
A policy that excluded African American players from organized baseball in the United States before 1946. *Baseball's color line was broken when Jackie Robinson signed up to play with the Brooklyn Dodgers.*

come•back
(**kuhm**-bak) *noun*
A return to popularity or success. *The band is making a comeback after 20 years.*

com•mand
(kuh-**mand**) *verb*
To order someone to do something. *You must command the dog to sit before giving it a treat.*

com•mit•ment
(kuh-**mit**-muhnt) *noun*
A promise to do or support something and to remain dedicated to it. *Carson made a commitment to eating a vegetarian diet.*

com•pa•ny
(**kuhm**-puh-nee) *noun*
A group of people who work together to produce or sell products or services. *Josh's mom works for a company that makes cars.*

Glossary continued**continued**

com•pass
(**kuhm**-puhss) *noun*
1. An instrument for finding directions, with a magnetic needle that always points north. *You can use a compass to follow a route on a map.*
2. An instrument that has two legs connected by a flexible joint, used for drawing circles. *My compass is a useful tool for helping me in geometry class.*

compass

com•plain
(kuhm-**playn**) *verb*
To say that you are unhappy about something. *Isabella decided to complain to the teacher about the noisy students.*

com•plex
1. (**kom**-pleks) *noun*
A group of buildings that are close together and are used for a particular purpose. *Our hockey team uses one of the rinks at the sports complex.*
2. (kuhm-**pleks**) *adjective*
Very complicated. *The instructions were complex and hard to understand.*

com•pos•er
(kuhm-**po**-zer) *noun*
A person who writes music. *Beethoven is a well-known classical music composer.*

com•pute
(kuhm-**pyoot**) *verb*
To find an answer by using mathematics; to calculate. *It was hard to compute how much each person owed for the dinner bill.*

con•cen•trate
(**kon**-suhn-trate) *verb*
To focus your thoughts and attention on something. *Jasmine had to concentrate to hear what her coach was saying over the loud noise.*

con•crete
(**kon**-kreet or kon-**kreet**) *noun*
A building material made from a mixture of sand, gravel, cement, and water. *The skateboard park half-pipe is made of concrete.*

con•fi•dence
(**kon**-fuh-duhnse) *noun*
Strong belief in your own or someone else's abilities. *We have confidence in your ability to get the project done on time.*

con•front
(kuhn-**fruhnt**) *verb*
To meet or face someone in a threatening or accusing way. *Justin decided to confront the boys who were saying mean things about him.*

con•stel•la•tion
(kon-stuh-**lay**-shuhn) *noun*
A group of stars that forms a shape or pattern and is named. *I saw the constellation Orion in the night sky.*

con•struct
(kuhn-**struhkt**) *verb*
To build or make something. *The state plans to construct three new bridges next year.*

con•struc•tion
(kuhn-**struhk**-shun) *noun*
The process of building or making something. *The road was closed because of construction on the new overpass.*

con•tem•plate
(**kon**-tuhm-plate) *verb*
To think seriously about something or to look at something thoughtfully. *The counselor suggested that Matthew contemplate applying for college.*

con•tent•ment
(kuhn-**tent**-ment) *noun*
A feeling of happiness and satisfaction. *He found contentment by living a simple life in the country.*

con•trap•tion
(kuhn-**trap**-shuhn) *noun*
A strange or odd device or machine. *The inventor created a funny contraption to perform tasks around his house.*

con•tri•bute
(kuhn-**trib**-yoot) *verb*
To give help or money to a person or an organization. *The charity asked our family to contribute some money to the winter fund drive.*

co•or•di•na•tion
(koh-**or**-duh-nay-shun) *noun*
Having good control in moving your arms and legs. *Salsa dancing takes good coordination by both partners.*

corn•y
(**korn**-ee) *adjective*
Very silly, simple, and sentimental. *My grandfather tells corny jokes that I've heard a million times before.*

cor•set
(**kor**-set) *noun*
A type of tightly fitting women's underwear worn in the past to shape the upper body. *In the 1800s a woman would wear a corset to make her waist smaller.*

corset

co-work•er
(**koh**-wurk-uhr) *noun*
Someone who works with someone else. *Isaiah's co-worker helped him finish the monthly report for their boss.*

cra•dle
(**kray**-duhl) *noun*
A small bed for a young baby. *My dad set up a cradle in the bedroom for the new baby to sleep in.*

cramp
(**kramp**) *noun*
Pain caused by a muscle tightening suddenly. *The basketball player had to come off the court because he got a cramp in his leg.*

Glossary continued

cra•ter
(**kray**-tur) *noun*
The open top of a volcano. *We hiked all the way up the volcano and looked down into the crater.*

crave
(**krave**) *verb*
To really want something. *Sometimes, I really crave strawberries.*

cre•a•tiv•i•ty
(kree-ay-**tiv**-uh-tee) *noun*
The ability to use your imagination and to be good at thinking of new ideas. *Art classes often help students develop their creativity.*

cri•tic
(**krit**-ik) *noun*
A person who writes reviews of books, movies, plays, or concerts. *The music critic from the newspaper wrote about the concert.*

crum•pled
(**kruhm**-puhl-d) *adjective*
Crushed into wrinkles and folds. *I never make my bed, so I always have crumpled sheets.*

curb
(**kurb**)
1. *noun*
A raised border along the edge of a paved street. *A red curb means you cannot park in that spot.*
2. *verb*
To control or hold back something. *Kit's mom said she must curb her time spent watching TV.*

cush•y
(**kush**-ee) *adjective*
Comfortable. *My shoes are so cushy, I could walk forever!*

cym•bal
(**sim**-buhl) *noun*
A musical instrument made of brass and shaped like a plate, played by hitting it with a stick or another cymbal. *The band's drummer ended the song by banging on the cymbal with his drumstick.*

cymbal

dash
(**dash**) *noun*
1. A short, quick run. *I made a dash to the phone so I would not miss the call.*
2. A horizontal line (—) used as a punctuation mark to show a pause in a sentence. *The whale was huge—and it was only a baby.*

de•com•pose
(dee-kuhm-**poze**) *verb*
To rot or decay. *After autumn leaves fall to the ground, they begin to decompose.*

de•fense
(di-**fenss**) *noun*
Something that is used for protection against something else. *The bear uses its claws as a defense when it feels threatened.*

den•si•ty
(**den**-si-tee) *noun*
The density of an object is how heavy or light it is for its size. *This small rock has a greater density than this button.*

de•pres•sion
(di-**presh**-uhn) *noun*
The state of feeling very sad or gloomy. *Losing the game sent Robert into a depression.*

des•ert
(**dez**-urt) *noun*
A dry, often sandy area where hardly any plants grow because there is so little rain. *Creatures and plants that live in the desert are able to live without much water.*

de•sign
(dih-**zahyn**)
1. *noun*
The shape or style of something. *The floor design had diamonds and squares.*
2. *verb*
To draw something that could be built or made. *Flora hired the architect to design her new house.*

de•vice
(di-**visse**) *noun*
A piece of equipment that does a particular job. *The computer is a device with many functions.*

dig•i•tal
(**dij**-uh-tuhl) *adjective*
Using a system for recording text, images, or sound in a form that can be used on a computer. *With a digital camera, you never need film.*

dis•a•bil•i•ty
(diss-uh-**bil**-uh-tee) *noun*
A physical or mental condition that makes it hard for someone to do things. *Brandon is blind, but he doesn't let his disability stop him from traveling.*

dis•as•ter
(duh-**zass**-tur) *noun*
An event that causes great damage, loss, or suffering, such as a flood or a serious train wreck. *Hurricane Katrina was a terrible disaster for the city of New Orleans— many homes were destroyed.*

dis•mayed
(diss-**made**) *adjective*
Upset and worried about something. *Kaylin was dismayed when she broke her leg before the big soccer game.*

dodge
(**doj**) *verb*
To avoid something or somebody by moving quickly. *Alyssa had to dodge the wild pitch or else the ball would hit her.*

doze
(**doze**) *verb*
To sleep lightly for a short time. *My Uncle Pete will sometimes doze off– but he'll wake up if you nudge him.*

earth•quake
(**urth**-kwayk) *noun*
A sudden violent shaking of the earth's surface, caused by a shifting of the earth's crust. *The earthquake this morning caused many of our dishes to fall off the shelf and break.*

ed•i•ble
(**ed**-uh-buhl) *adjective*
Able to be eaten. *When I lived in Japan, I sometimes ate edible flowers in restaurants.*

el•der•ly
(**el**-dur-lee) *adjective*
Old. *The elderly man was 90 when he won the dance contest.*

el•e•va•tion
(el-uh-**vay**-shuhn) *noun*
The height above sea
level. *We camped in the
mountains at an elevation
of 8,000 feet.*

elevation

e•lim•i•nate
(i-**lim**-uh-nate) *verb*
To leave out or to get rid
of. *Let's try to eliminate
pollution from the planet.*

en•er•gy
(**en**-ur-jee) *noun*
1. The strength to do
active things without
getting tired. *Eating a
granola bar gave me
energy to finish the hike.*
2. Power from coal,
electricity, or other
sources that makes
machines work and
produces heat. *The coal
plant produces enough
energy to heat all the
town's homes.*

en•vi•ron•ment
(en-**vye**-ruhn-muhnt)
noun
The natural world of
the land, sea, and air.
*Pollution is harming the
environment.*

en•vy
(**en**-vee) *verb*
To wish you could have
what another person
has, or do something he
or she has done. *I envy
that she worked hard and
finished in first place.*

e•quip•ment
(i-**kwip**-muhnt) *noun*
The tools and machines
needed for a particular
purpose or activity.
*Construction equipment
includes hammers, saws,
nails, and bulldozers.*

ev•i•dence
(**ev**-uh-duhnss) *noun*
Information or facts
that prove something is
true. *There was strong
evidence that the man
committed the crime.*

e•volve
(i-**volv**) *verb*
To develop an idea or
plan by making changes
to current ideas or plans.
*Many modern dances
have evolved from older
forms of dance.*

ex•cel
(ek-**sel**) *verb*
To do something very
well. *Tim and Nick excel
at basketball because
they practice every day.*

ex•per•i•ment
(ek-**sper**-uh-ment)
1. *verb*
To try something
new. *She decided to
experiment with different
ingredients to create the
perfect recipe.*
2. *noun*
A scientific test to try out
a theory or to see the
effect of something. *Our
experiment in science
class used magnets.*

experiment

ex•plore
(ek-**splor**) *verb*
To discover what a place is like. *The American tourists were eager to explore Paris.*

ex•treme•ly
(ek-**streem**-lee) *adverb*
To a great degree. *Nancy's puppy is extremely cute.*

fad
(**fad**) *noun*
Something that is very popular for a short time. *I cannot keep up with every fad, so I just buy things that I like.*

fash•ion•a•ble
(**fash**-uhn-uh-buhl) *adjective*
Popular at a certain time. *Flannel shirts were fashionable in the early 1990s.*

fate
(**fayt**) *noun*
What becomes of a person or a thing. *The fate of the fish depends on if the lake will dry up.*

feel like a mil•lion bucks
(**feel like uh mil**-yuhn **buhks**)
idiom
To feel great. *Having just scored the winning goal, I feel like a million bucks.*

fil•ter
(**fil**-tur) *verb*
To put liquids or gases through a device that cleans them. *We always filter stream water when we're hiking so that we do not get sick.*

fine
(**fine**)
1. *noun*
A sum of money paid as punishment for doing something wrong. *She paid a fine to the library for returning her book late.*
2. *adjective*
Very good, excellent, or of high quality. *The prince always wore fine clothing made with expensive fabrics.*

fleet
(**fleet**) *noun*
A number of ships, planes, or cars that form a group. *A fleet of taxis waited outside the train station for passengers.*

flim•sy
(**flim**-zee) *adjective*
Thin or weak. *I don't trust that flimsy table to hold this heavy pot.*

flop
(**flop**) *noun*
Something that is a failure. *The play was a flop because no one liked it.*

fly•er
(**flye**-uhr) *noun*
A piece of paper advertising something. *We saw a flyer announcing the band's concert next week.*

fore•cast
(**for**-kast) *noun*
To guess what is likely to happen in the future, based on current information. *The weather forecast calls for rain tomorrow.*

Glossary

for•eign
(**for**-uhn) *adjective*
To do with or coming from another country. *Beth likes seeing foreign films because she wants to learn Spanish.*

foun•da•tion
(foun-**day**-shuhn)
1. *noun*
A solid structure on which a building is built. *The tornado blew away all but the foundation of the house.*
2. *noun*
An organization that gives money to worthwhile causes. *Each year, the foundation gives money to promising student writers.*

fun•gus
(**fuhn**-guhss) *noun*
A simple plantlike organism with no leaves, flowers, or roots that grows in dark, warm, moist places. *A mushroom is a type of fungus.*

fungus

gad•get
(**gaj**-it) *noun*
A small tool that does a particular job. *We have a gadget for slicing eggs.*

gal•ax•y
(**gal**-uhk-see) *noun*
A very large group of stars and planets. *Earth is in the Milky Way galaxy.*

gem
(**jem**) *noun*
A precious stone such as a diamond, a ruby, or an emerald. *Her grandmother gave her a ring with a sparkling gem.*

gob•ble
(**gob**-uhl) *verb*
To eat food quickly. *Make sure the dog does not gobble down its food.*

grav•i•ty
(**grav**-uh-tee) *noun*
The force that pulls things down toward the surface of the earth and keeps them from floating away into space. *If you jump, the earth's gravity will pull you back down.*

green•house
(**green**-houss) *noun*
A glass building in which you grow plants and protect them from the weather. *We can control the temperature in our greenhouse, which allows us to grow flowers all year long.*

hack
(**hak**) *verb*
To illegally get into a computer system. *Someone tried to hack into my brother's email account to gain information without his permission.*

hand•writ•ten
(**hand**-rit-tuhn) *noun*
Written by a person (not a machine), with a pen or pencil. *I prefer receiving a handwritten note rather than an email.*

hang glid•ing
(**hang glide**-ing) *noun*
The sport of flying using an aircraft like a giant kite with a harness for a pilot hanging below it. *Katie loves the freedom she feels as she sails through the air while hang gliding.*

hard•ship
(**hard**-ship) *noun*
Difficulty or suffering. *Our family faced hardship when our mom lost her job last year.*

hare
(**hair**) *noun*
An animal like a large rabbit with long, strong back legs. *The dog chased the hare across the field, but the hare was able to outrun him.*

har•ness
(**har**-niss)
1. *noun*
An arrangement of straps used to keep someone safe. *Jan made sure her harness was secure before she parachuted out of the plane.*
2. *noun*
A set of leather straps and metal pieces that connect a horse or another animal to a plow, cart, or wagon. *The horse's harness broke and the wagon rolled back down the hill.*

harness

har•vest
(**har**-vest)
1. *verb*
To collect or gather up crops. *Fred was able to harvest more corn this year than he did last year.*
2. *noun*
The crops themselves. *The growing season was good, so we expect a healthy harvest this fall.*

health•y
(**hel**-thee) *adjective*
Good for your body or mind. *Apples are part of a healthy diet.*

hes•i•tant
(**hehz**-uh-tuhnt) *adjective*
Doubtful, undecided. *Laura was hesitant about which new CD to buy.*

hoax
(**hohks**) *noun*
A trick or a practical joke that makes someone believe something that is false. *The news that aliens had landed on Earth turned out to be a hoax.*

home run
(**home run**) *noun*
In baseball, a hit that allows the batter to run all the way around the bases and score a run. *The baseball player hit a game-winning home run.*

hon•or
(**on**-ur) *noun*
A special privilege or award that makes you feel proud. *The President said that it was an honor to visit our town.*

il•le•gal
(i-**lee**-guhl) *adjective*
Against the law. *Stealing is illegal.*

im•ag•ine
(i-**maj**-uhn) *verb*
To picture something in your mind. *When it is really cold outside, sometimes I imagine I am lounging on a warm beach.*

Glossary

im•mi•grant
(**im**-uh-gruhnt) *noun*
Someone who comes from one country to live permanently in another country. *My father is an immigrant who came from Ireland to live in the United States.*

im•press
(im-**press**) *verb*
To make people think highly of you. *David hopes to impress his teacher by doing extra credit work.*

in a flash
(**in** uh flash) *idiom*
Very quickly. *I called Dad for help and he was there in a flash.*

in a huff
(**in** uh huhf) *idiom*
Feeling upset or very annoyed. *Jay got mad at his sister and left in a huff.*

in a jam
(**in** uh jam) *idiom*
Difficult situation. *Jeff was in a terrible jam—he'd gone to take his test without a pencil.*

in a rut
(**in** uh ruht) *idiom*
Always doing something in the same boring way. *Hank was stuck in a rut with his breakfast routine—he ate a bowl of the same cereal every morning.*

in•cred•i•ble
(in-**kred**-uh-buhl) *adjective*
Unbelievable, amazing, or very good. *Jack's beanstalk grew to an incredible size.*

in•hab•it
(in-**hab**-it) *verb*
To live in a place. *If the boy becomes king, then he will inhabit the castle.*

in•still
(in-**stil**) *verb*
To put into one's mind slowly, over a period of time. *Teachers at John's school instill pride in their students.*

in•ter•na•tion•al
(in-tur-**nash**-uh-nuhl) *adjective*
Involving more than one country. *The international-news reporter explained what was happening around the world.*

in•ven•tion
(in-**ven**-shuhn) *noun*
A process or device that has been created or made for the first time. *The telephone was an invention that made it possible for people to talk to others who were far away.*

jolt
(**johlt**) *verb*
To move with sudden rough jerks. *The earthquake jolted San Francisco.*

jug•gle
(**juhg**-uhl) *verb*
To keep three or more balls, clubs, or other objects moving through the air by repeatedly throwing them up and catching them again, one after the other. *The clown can juggle four balls without dropping any of them.*

key•board
(**kee**-bord) *noun*
The set of keys on a computer, typewriter, piano, etc. *Carolyn took a class to learn the order of the letters on the computer keyboard, so she could type faster.*

kib•ble
(**ki**-buhl) *noun*
Ground beans or grain shaped into little pieces, especially for pet food. *The police dogs always have a big bowl of kibble waiting for them when they come back from patrol.*

lar•va
(**lar**-vuh) *noun*
An insect at a stage of development after being an egg and before becoming an adult insect. *A caterpillar is the larva of a moth or a butterfly.*

larva

lev•ee
(**lev**-ee) *noun*
A wall built up near a river to prevent flooding. *After the river flooded our town, the state government voted to build a levee to hold back the water.*

light•house
(**lite**-houss) *noun*
A tower in or near the sea that has a flashing light at the top to guide ships or warn them of danger. *When it is foggy, a lighthouse lets ships know where land is, so they don't crash into it.*

like•ness
(**like**-nuhs) *noun*
A picture or portrait. *That painting is a very good likeness of my grandfather.*

limb
(**lim**) *noun*
A body part used for moving or grasping. *Arms, legs, wings, and flippers are limbs.*

liq•uid
(**lik**-wid) *noun*
A wet substance that can flow or be poured. *When ice melts, it turns from a solid into a liquid that you can drink.*

lo•cal
(**loh**-kuhl) *adjective*
Near your house or having to do with the area where you live. *We get the local newspaper to tell us about events around town.*

Lux•em•bourg
(**luhks**-uhm-berg) *noun*
A country in western Europe between Belgium and Germany. *My family plans to visit Luxembourg this summer when we travel to Europe.*

Luxembourg

maj•es•tic
(muh-**jess**-tik) *adjective*
Having great power and beauty. *The ocean is majestic during a storm.*

**make a splash
(make uh splash)**
idiom
To have or create an exciting effect or event. *Her clothing designs made a splash in the fashion world.*

**make it plain
(make it plane)** *idiom*
To communicate something to someone in a clear and simple way. *Seth believes that his actions will make it plain that he was telling the truth.*

mam•mal
(**mam**-uhl) *noun*
A warm-blooded animal with a backbone. Female mammals produce milk to feed their young. *Humans, cows, and dolphins are mammals.*

mam•moth
(**mam**-uhth)
1. *noun*
An extinct animal that resembles a large elephant, with long, curved tusks and shaggy hair. *We saw the bones of a mammoth at the natural history museum.*
2. *adjective*
Huge. *Building a skyscraper is a mammoth task.*

man•age
(**man**-ij) *verb*
1. To be able to do something that is difficult or awkward. *Can you manage carrying all those bags?*
2. To be in charge of. *Terry will manage the store.*

man•u•fac•tur•er
(man-yuh-**fak**-chur-ur) *noun*
A person or business that makes something, often with machines. *Maria's cell phone broke, so she sent it back to the manufacturer to be fixed.*

mer•chant
(**mur**-chuhnt) *adjective*
Of or relating to the trade and sale of goods. *A country's merchant marine is made of ships and crews that carry goods for trade.*

me•te•or
(**mee**-tee-ur) *noun*
A piece of rock or metal from space that enters the earth's atmosphere at high speed, burns, and forms a streak of light. *When you see a shooting star in the night sky, you are seeing a meteor.*

mi•cro•light plane
(**mye**-kroh-lyt **plane**)
noun
A small, lightweight, inexpensive plane that flies slowly at low altitude. *My aunt's hobby is to fly microlight planes.*

Mid•dle East
(**mid**-uhl **eest**) *noun*
A large region made up of parts of southwestern Asia and northern Africa, and includes countries such as Iran, Iraq, Israel, Saudi Arabia, and Egypt. *Many languages are spoken in the Middle East, but Arabic is the most common.*

Middle East

mid•town
(**mid**-town) *noun*
The central part of a city. *He wants to live in midtown so he will be close to his job.*

mi•grate
(**mye**-grate) *verb*
To move from one country, region, or climate to another. *Many animals migrate to warmer regions when the climate becomes cold.*

min•er
(**mine**-uhr) *noun*
A person who digs up minerals that are underground. *The miner dug deep to find gold.*

mole•hill
(**mohl**-hil) *noun*
A small mound of earth created by a mole, a small furry mammal. *My brother discovered a molehill in our backyard.*

moon•light
(**moon**-lite) *noun*
The light of the moon that you can see at night. *I don't need a flashlight when there is a full moon because I can see by moonlight.*

nau•se•a
(**naw**-zee-uh or **naw**-zhuh) *noun*
A feeling of being sick to your stomach. *I got nausea from riding in a boat when there were big waves.*

nerve
(**nurv**) *noun*
A thin fiber that sends messages between your brain or spinal cord and other parts of your body so that you can move and feel. *Miles damaged a nerve in his thumb and had trouble feeling hot and cold.*

Neth•er•lands
(**neh**-thur-landz) *noun*
A country in western Europe on the North Sea where the Dutch language is spoken. *The Netherlands is a country famous for its windmills, tulips, and the city of Amsterdam.*

Netherlands

Glossary continued

nib•ble

(**nib**-uhl) *verb*

To bite something gently, or to take small bites of something. *The zookeeper watched the rabbit nibble on its carrot.*

niece

(**neess**) *noun*

The daughter of your brother or sister, or the daughter of your husband's or wife's brother or sister. *I am babysitting my niece so that my sister has time to go shopping.*

not to be tak•en se•ri•ous•ly

(**not too bee tayk-**uhn **sihr**-ee-uhss-lee) *idiom*

To not understand or consider something in a certain way. *His threats to quit are not to be taken seriously. He has said that many times before and is still with the band.*

nov•e•list

(**nov**-uh-list) *noun*

A person who writes books about made-up people and events. *A novelist came to my school to talk about a new book she wrote.*

ob•ject

(**ob**-jekt) *noun*

Something that you can see and touch but is not alive. *An object was placed on the table.*

of•fense

1. (uh-**fenss**) *noun*

The act of upsetting or angering someone. *Jane didn't mean to cause offense to Tom when she said his story was boring.*

2. (**aw**-fenss) *noun*

In sports, the team that is attacking or trying to score. *Our offense had two minutes to make a touchdown or we would lose the football game.*

off-key

(**awf-kee**) ad*verb*

Out of tune. *The songs sound bad because the piano plays off-key.*

on the edge of my seat

(**on thuh ej ov mye seet**) *idiom*

Excited and paying full attention to something. *I was on the edge of my seat waiting to see if the acrobat would fall.*

o•pin•ion

(uh-**pin**-yuhn) *noun*

The ideas and beliefs that you have about something. *What's your opinion of our new teacher?*

ore

(**or**) *noun*

A rock that contains metal. *While exploring the deep cave, the geologists discovered it was filled with iron ore.*

or•gan
(**or**-guhn) *noun*
1. A part of the body that does a particular job. *The heart is the organ that pumps blood through the body.*
2. A large musical instrument like a piano, with large pipes. *I play the organ in choir while others sing along.*

organ

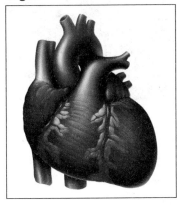

or•ga•nism
(**or**-guh-niz-uhm) *noun*
A living plant or animal. *Scientists studied the life cycle of the organism.*

out•break
(**out**-brake) *noun*
A sudden start of something bad, such as disease or war. *Every year people get shots to prevent an outbreak of the flu.*

out•dat•ed
(out-**day**-tid) *adjective*
Old-fashioned or out of date. *Typewriters are becoming outdated.*

ox•y•gen
(**ok**-suh-juhn) *noun*
A colorless gas found in the air. *All plants and animals need oxygen to live.*

pad•dle
(**pad**-uhl) *verb*
To move and steer through water using your hands or a short, wide pole called a paddle. *We had to paddle our boat across the lake to the dock.*

parch•ment
(**parch**-muhnt) *noun*
Heavy material made from the skin of sheep or goats and used for writing on. *The Declaration of Independence was written on parchment.*

pas•sion
(**pash**-uhn) *noun*
Strong liking or enthusiasm for something. *Greg has a passion for historic cars.*

pay the price
(**pay thuh prisse**)
idiom
To accept the consequences of an action or behavior. *Ken did not study for his math test, and now he will pay the price.*

pen•i•cil•lin
(pen-uh-**sil**-uhn) *noun*
A drug made from a mold that helps fight some diseases by killing bacteria. *The doctor gave me some penicillin to help me get better when I was sick.*

phrase
(**fraze**) *noun*
A group of words that have a meaning but do not form a sentence. *"In the dark" is a phrase.*

pick•y
(**pik**-ee) *adjective*
Fussy or choosy, difficult to make happy. *Juan is so picky about his clothes—he will only shop at two stores.*

Glossary continued

pi•rate
(**pye**-rit) *noun*
Someone who attacks and steals from ships at sea. *The ship's captain was afraid of being attacked and robbed by pirates.*

pitch
(**pich**) *verb*
To throw or toss something, such as a baseball. *The batter could not hit Jose's fast pitch.*

plop
(**plop**) *verb*
To sit, drop, or fall down heavily. *When I am tired, I like to plop down on the couch and watch TV.*

plunk down
(**pluhnk down**) *verb*
To spend a lot of money for something. *Bryan will need to plunk down a lot of cash to purchase that car.*

pol•i•tics
(**pol**-uh-tiks) *noun*
The ideas, debate, and activity involved in governing a country. *Emma is involved in state politics.*

pol•len
(**pol**-uhn) *noun*
Yellow powder found in flowers, which is carried on the wind or by insects to make other flowers produce seeds. *In the spring, there is lots of pollen in the air.*

post•pone
(pohst-**pone**) *verb*
To delay something until later or another time. *We will postpone the picnic because it is raining.*

pre•cau•tion
(pre-**kaw**-shuhn) *noun*
Something you do to prevent something bad from happening. *Let's take along a first-aid kit as a precaution.*

pre•cinct
(**pree**-singkt) *noun*
A police station in an area. *My aunt is a police officer at the local precinct.*

pred•a•tor
(**pred**-uh-tur) *noun*
An animal that lives by hunting other animals for food. *A shark is a predator that lives in the ocean.*

predator

pre•dict
(pri-**dikt**) *verb*
To say what you think may happen in the future. *Can you predict tomorrow's weather?*

prey
(**pray**) *noun*
An animal that is hunted by another animal for food. *Mice are the prey of owls and other hunters.*

pro•cess
(**pross**-ess) *noun*
An organized series of actions that produces a result. *Manny's process for writing his report involved research, interviewing experts, and following his teacher's writing guidelines.*

pro•duce
1. (**proh**-dooss) *noun*
Things that are produced or grown for eating. *We went to the produce area of the store to find fruits and vegetables.*
2. (pruh-**dooss**) *verb*
To make something. *The new factory will produce cars.*

prof•it
(**prof**-it) *noun*
The amount of money left after all the costs of running a business have been subtracted from all the money earned. *We had a profit of $5,000 after paying our bills.*

prone
(**prohn**) *adjective*
1. Likely to act, feel, or be a certain way. *Joe is prone to mischief.*
2. Lying flat or face down. *The patient was lying prone on the hospital bed.*

prowl
(**proul**) *verb*
To move around quietly and secretly. *Many animals prowl at night in search of food.*

pub•li•shing
(**puhb**-lish-ing) *noun*
The business or activity of writing, printing, and distributing books, magazines, newspapers, or other materials. *Since Caleb loves to write, he would love to work in the publishing industry one day.*

pulse
(**puhlss**) *noun*
A steady beat or throb, such as the feeling of the heart moving blood through the body. *The doctor checked the injured man's pulse.*

punch line
(**puhnch line**) *noun*
The last line of a joke or story that makes it funny or surprising. *My aunt always forgets the punch line and ruins the joke.*

push•cart
(**push**-kart) *noun*
A light wagon that is pushed by someone and is used to carry heavy items, such as groceries. *The man sold fruit from a pushcart.*

pushcart

Glossary continued

ra•di•o code
(**ray**-dee-oh **kode**) *noun*
A system of words, letters, symbols, or numbers used instead of ordinary words to send messages by radio. *The policeman heard the radio code that told him there was a robbery taking place.*

rec•i•pe
(**ress**-i-pee) *noun*
Instructions for preparing and cooking food. *My mom has the best recipe for bran muffins.*

rec•ord
1. (**rek**-urd) *noun*
The best performance ever, such as the fastest speed or longest distance in a sport. *The athlete set the record for highest jump.*
2. (ri-**kord**) *verb*
To put music or other sounds onto a tape, compact disk, or record. *The student was able to record himself while reading.*

re•cy•cle
(ree-**sye**-kuhl) *verb*
To process used items in order to make new products. *In our city we recycle glass, plastic, newspapers, and cans instead of throwing them away.*

reed
(**reed**) *noun*
1. A piece of thin wood, metal, or plastic in some musical instruments that makes a sound when you blow over it. *The clarinet, oboe, and saxophone are instruments that have a reed.*
2. A tall grass that grows in or near water. *The ducks hide in the reeds near the water.*

re•mains
(ri-**maynz**) *noun plural*
Parts of something that was once alive. *Judging by the animal remains, Scott concluded a wolf had entered the area.*

re•search
(**ree**-surch) *verb*
To study and find out about a subject, usually by reading a lot of books about it or by doing experiments. *Ariel had to research the Civil War for her school project.*

re•sist
(ri-**zist**) *verb*
To stop yourself from doing something that you would like to do. *It is hard to resist sleeping on a rainy day.*

rink
(**ringk**) *noun*
An area with a specially prepared surface that is used for ice-skating, roller-skating, or hockey. *We decided to go skating at the outdoor rink.*

ripe
(**ripe**) *adjective*
Ready to be harvested, picked, or eaten. *Ripe strawberries taste sweeter than unripe ones.*

riv•et

(**riv**-it) *noun*

A strong metal bolt that is used to fasten pieces of metal or fabric together. *The mechanic used a rivet to hold a section of the car together.*

rivet

roar

(**ror**) *verb*

To make a loud, deep noise. *The crowd roared when the team scored.*

rook•ie

(**ruk**-ee) *noun*

Someone who has just joined a group and has little experience and training. *The fire station hired a new rookie who has a lot to learn.*

roy•al•ty

(**roi**-uhl-tee) *noun*

1. A king or queen, or someone who belongs to the family of a king or queen. *In my new dress, I felt like royalty.*

2. A payment made to an author, composer, or inventor for each item or copy of a work sold. *A jazz musician earns a royalty each time you buy a CD.*

sat•el•lite

(**sat**-uh-lite) *noun*

A machine that has been sent into space and travels around the earth, moon, stars, etc. *A communications satellite can send television and telephone signals to earth.*

say•ing

(**say**-ing) *noun*

A short, well-known phrase or expression that gives advice. *"Don't cry over spilt milk" is a saying that means not to worry about something if it has already happened.*

scar•ring

(**skar**-ing) *noun*

Marks left on skin by a cut or wound that has healed. *She was left with scarring on her face after the burns healed.*

sched•ule

(**skej**-ul) *noun*

A plan, program, or timetable. *My science teacher doesn't have any time in his schedule to meet with me this week.*

sci•ence fair

(**sye**-uhnss **fair**) *noun*

A competition where students create projects related to science or technology. *Ayesha won first place at the science fair for her volcano exhibit.*

sci•en•tist

(**sye**-uhn-tist) *noun*

Someone who studies nature and the physical world by testing, experimenting, and measuring. *Laura wants to be a scientist so she can find new types of energy.*

scowl
(**skoul**) *verb*
To frown in an angry manner. *Missing her bus made Nola scowl.*

scribe
(**skribe**) *noun*
A person who copies books, letters, and other documents by writing them. *In past times, people would hire a scribe to make them a copy of a book.*

scribe

seg•ment
(**seg**-muhnt) *noun*
A part or section of something. *Lucy divided the orange and ate it one segment at a time.*

self-suf•fi•cient
(self-suh-**fish**-uhnt) *adjective*
Able to take care of one's own needs without help from others. *When Germaine got her driver's license, she became more self-sufficient.*

sense
(**senss**) *noun*
1. One of the powers a living being uses to learn about its surroundings: sight, hearing, touch, taste, and smell. *The dog used its strong sense of hearing to listen for intruders.*
2. Good judgment. *Greg has the sense to eat a healthy breakfast each morning.*

ser•ies
(**sihr**-eez) *noun*
A group of related things that follow in order. *I took a series of swimming lessons last summer.*

shot
(**shot**)
1. *adjective*
To be useless or destroyed. *This light bulb is shot—do we have another one?*
2. *noun*
An injection. *I got a flu shot before the winter.*

shrub
(**shruhb**) *noun*
A small plant or bush. *The yard was plain, so we planted a shrub along the driveway.*

side•line
(**side**-line) *noun*
A line that marks the edges of the playing area in sports, such as football, basketball, and soccer. *The soccer ball was kicked out of bounds at the sideline.*

sin•is•ter
(**sin**-uh-stur) *adjective*
Seeming evil and threatening. *I covered my ears whenever I heard the character's sinister laugh.*

Sis•tine Chap•el
(**sis**-teen **chap**-uhl) *noun*
A chapel in Rome that has a famous painted ceiling. *An artist named Michelangelo painted the ceiling of the Sistine Chapel.*

sky•scrap•er
(**skye**-skray-pur) *noun*
A very tall building. *The new skyscraper will be the tallest building in the city.*

skyscraper

smug•gle
(**smuhg**-uhl) *verb*
To sneak or move something from one place to another, often illegally. *We had to smuggle Jim's present into the house.*

snarl
(**snarl**) *verb*
For an animal to show its teeth and make a growling sound. *I knew the dog would snarl if I surprised it while it was eating.*

snow•shoe
(**snoh**-shoo) *noun*
A webbed frame that is shaped like a racket that helps you walk on snow. *When my left snowshoe fell off, I felt my left foot sink into the snow.*

so•ci•e•ty
(suh-**sye**-uh-tee) *noun*
All the people who live in the same country or area and share the same laws and customs. *Laws are made to protect a society.*

soggy
(**sog**-ee) *adjective*
Very wet or soaked. *My shoes were soggy from walking in the rain.*

soothe
(**sooth**) *verb*
1. To relieve something that is painful or uncomfortable. *This cream should soothe your rash.*
2. To calm someone who is angry or upset. *Fran tried to soothe the screaming baby.*

spare
(**spair**) *verb*
1. *verb*
To give or make something available. *Can you spare a few minutes?*
2. *adjective*
Extra and kept for use when needed. *I keep a spare tire in my car in case I get a flat.*

spear
(**spihr**) *noun*
A weapon with a long handle and a pointed head. *A spear can be used to catch a fish.*

spe•cial ef•fect
(**spesh**-uhl uh-**fekt**) *noun*
An image or sound used in film, television, and movies to represent imagined events in a story. *The science fiction movie often used a special effect to show a man flying.*

spe•cial•ist
(**spesh**-uh-list) *noun*
An expert at one particular job or area. *Her doctor is a specialist in heart disease.*

sprint
(**sprint**) *verb*
To run fast for a short distance. *Gerry had to sprint across the park so that he wouldn't be late for school.*

sta•ble
(**stay**-buhl)
1. *adjective*
Firm and steady. *Before you climb the ladder, make sure it is stable.*
2. *noun*
A building or part of a building where horses or cows are kept. *I put the horse back in the stable after my ride.*

sta•tion
(**stay**-shuhn) *noun*
A building or place that is a center for a type of service or activity. *The train station is crowded with people in the morning.*

sta•tus
(**stat**-uhss) *noun*
1. A person's rank or position in a group, organization, or society. *Some people like to show their status by buying a fancy car.*
2. The condition of a situation. *Do you know the status of her application?*

steep
(**steep**) *adjective*
Sharply sloping up or down. *Our house is on top of a steep hill.*

steep

strength
(**strengkth**) *noun*
The quality of being strong and having power. *I am building up my strength by lifting weights.*

stress out
(**stress out**) *phrasal verb*
To become so worried and tired that you cannot relax. *I often stress out before taking an important test.*

strik•ing
(**strike**-ing) *adjective*
Unusual or noticeable in some way. *My grandmother looks very striking in her new dress.*

stroke
(**strohk**) *noun*
1. A sudden illness where there is a lack of oxygen in part of the brain caused by the blocking or breaking of a blood vessel. *My grandpa had a stroke and now he can't move his left side.*
2. A way of moving in swimming or rowing, or of hitting the ball in tennis or golf. *Jim needed to practice his golf stroke to improve his game.*

stunt
(**stuhnt**) *noun*
An act that shows great skill or daring, done to show off or entertain. *The crowd cheered as the circus performer completed a dangerous stunt on the trapeze.*

sub•ject
(**suhb**-jikt) *noun*
The person or thing that is discussed in a book, article, or conversation. *Casey loved the book's subject.*

sub•let
(suhb-**leht**) *verb*
To rent a house or apartment for a short period of time. *The man sublet his apartment when he went away for two months.*

sup•pose
(suh-**poze**) *verb*
To expect. *I suppose the new television show will be popular.*

surf•board
(**surf**-bord) *noun*
A narrow board that you stand on to ride breaking waves. *Kai got water up his nose when he fell off his surfboard.*

surge
(**surj**) *verb*
To rush forward suddenly and powerfully. *The strong winds caused the water to surge against the shore.*

sur•prise
(sur-**prize**) *noun*
Something that is unexpected or amazing. *Alex's performance in the play was a surprise, since he can be quiet.*

sur•vi•vor
(sur-**vye**-vur) *noun*
Someone who lives through a disaster or horrible event. *The train crash survivor explained to the reporters how he was able to live through the disaster.*

sus•pect
1. (suh-**spekt**) *verb*
To think that something may be true; to guess or suppose. *I suspect that David is late because he woke up late.*
2. (**suhss**-pekt) *noun*
Someone thought to be responsible for a crime. *Jan is a suspect in the robbery last week.*

sus•pense
(suh-**spenss**) *noun*
An anxious and uncertain feeling caused by having to wait to see what happens. *We were all in suspense as we waited to learn the winners of the contest.*

Glossary continued

sys•tem
(**siss**-tuhm) *noun*
An orderly way of doing something; a method. *I need a better system for studying.*

taint
(**taynt**) *verb*
To spoil or pollute. *We must stop the flow of the chemicals that taint our lakes and rivers.*

ta•ran•tu•la
(tuh-**ran**-chuh-luh) *noun*
A large hairy spider found mainly in warm areas. *Michelle screamed when she saw the tarantula crawling across the floor.*

tarantula

team•mate
(**teem**-mate) *noun*
A fellow member of a team. *Derek passed the ball to his teammate, who then made a basket.*

team•work
(**teem**-wurk) *noun*
The labor or effort of two or more people acting together to get something done. *Winning a basketball game takes teamwork.*

tech•no•lo•gy
(tek-**nol**-uh-jee) *noun*
The use of science to do practical things. *Cell phones are a useful technology.*

tem•per•a•ture
(**tem**-pur-uh-chur) *noun*
The amount of heat or cold in something, measured by degrees. *The temperature is often high during the day and low at night in the desert.*

ten•dril
(**ten**-dril) *noun*
A long, thin curling piece of something such as hair or the stem of a plant. *Kathy twisted a tendril of hair around her finger.*

ten•ta•cle
(**ten**-tuh-kuhl) *noun*
One of the long, flexile arm-like parts of some animals, such as the octopus and squid. *A giant squid used its tentacles to grasp for food.*

ter•rain
(tuh-**rayn**) *noun*
Ground or land. *The terrain was very rocky.*

the•o•ry
(**thee**-ur-ee or **thihr**-ee) *noun*
An idea or statement that explains how or why something happens. *James had a theory about who may have eaten his lunch.*

thrash
(**thrash**) *verb*
To move wildly or violently. *The fish will thrash around on the dock after we take it off the hook.*

thrive
(**thrive**) *verb*
To grow and do well. *Roses thrive in our garden.*

tint
(**tint**) *noun*
A variety of a color, often one with white added. *The artist added a blue tint to the photograph.*

tor•na•do
(tor-**nay**-doh) *noun*
A violent whirling column of air that appears as a dark cloud shaped like a funnel. *A tornado travels quickly and usually destroys everything in its narrow path.*

tornado

track
(**trak**)
1. *noun*
The sport of running on a special surface. *Jake has track practice every day after school.*
2. *verb*
To follow someone or something. *The police officers used clues to track the thief.*

tra•di•tion
(truh-**dish**-uhn) *noun*
A custom, idea, or belief that is handed down from one generation to the next. *Our family's tradition is to trade pasta recipes.*

traf•fic
(**traf**-ik) *noun*
Moving vehicles. *There was a lot of traffic in the city this morning.*

trans•mit
(transs-**mit**) *verb*
1. To send or pass something from one place or person to another. *Cover your mouth when you sneeze so you don't transmit germs.*
2. To send out radio or television signals. *The program transmits on Fridays.*

trans•por•ta•tion
(transs-pur-**tay**-shuhn) *noun*
A way of moving people and goods from one place to another. *My bicycle is my main form of transportation.*

treas•ure
(**trezh**-ur) *noun*
Gold, jewels, money, or other valuable things that have been collected or hidden. *Jessica will use the old map to search for buried treasure.*

trend•y
(**trend**-ee) *adjective*
Modern and fashionable. *The color green was trendy in clothing this year.*

trib•ute
(**trib**-yoot) *noun*
Something done, given, or said to show thanks or respect. *The president's speech was a tribute to the soldiers who died in the war.*

tun•nel
(**tuhn**-uhl) *noun*
1. An animal's burrow. *The prairie dog ran down into its tunnel when it saw the eagle overhead.*
2. A passage built beneath the ground or water or through a mountain for use by cars, trains, or other vehicles. *The Channel Tunnel runs under the sea between England and France.*

tunnel

u•nique
(yoo-**neek**) *adjective*
One of a kind. *Every fingerprint is unique.*

un•sus•pect•ing
(uhn-suh-**spekt**-ing) *adjective*
Not knowing that something is about to happen.
Mr. Hernandez surprised his unsuspecting son with keys to the family car.

un•wise
(uhn-**wize**) *adjective*
Showing bad judgment; foolish. *Their unwise decision to drive in the snowstorm led to them crashing into a tree.*

up•date
(uhp-**date**)
1. *verb*
To change something in order to include the latest style or information, or to tell someone the latest information. *After years of wearing her hair in the same style, Jamie decided to update her look with a new haircut.*
2. *noun*
The latest news about something. *Doctor, please give me an update on the patient's condition.*

va•cant
(**vay**-kuhnt) *adjective*
Empty or not lived in. *The house has been vacant for several years.*

van•ish
(**van**-ish) *verb*
To disappear or cease to exist. *For his next trick, the magician will vanish before our eyes.*

ve•hi•cle
(**vee**-uh-kuhl) *noun*
Something in which people or goods are carried from one place to another. *A car is a type of vehicle.*

vend•ing ma•chine
(**vend**-ing muh-**sheen**) *noun*
A machine you put money into to buy food, beverage, or other products. *Can you get me a granola bar from the vending machine?*

ven•om
(**ven**-uhm) *noun*
Poison produced by some snakes and spiders. *Venom is usually passed into a victim's body through a bite or sting.*

vo•cab•u•lar•y
(voh-**kab**-yuh-ler-ee) *noun*
All of the words that a person uses and understands. *Charles impressed his teachers with his large vocabulary.*

vol•un•teer
(vol-uhn-**tihr**)
1. *noun*
Someone who offers to do a job, usually without pay. *The volunteer helped clean up the animal shelter.*
2. *verb*
To offer to do a job, usually without payment. *On Tuesday afternoons, I volunteer at the local hospital.*

wade
(**wayd**) *verb*
To walk through water. *I like to wade in the pool before I swim laps.*

wel•fare
(**wel**-fair) *noun*

A person or thing's state of health, happiness, and comfort. *For your own welfare, you should try to get more sleep.*

wreck
(**rek**)

1. *noun*
A bad accident, such as one involving cars, planes, or trains. *Traffic was slow because of the car wreck.*

2. *verb*
To destroy or ruin something. *You will wreck my dress if you spill juice on it!*

wreck

yield
(**yeeld**) *verb*
To surrender or give something up. *The defeated troops had to yield the town to their enemy.*

Credits

Cover (top to bottom; clockwise): © Jeremy Woodhouse/Photodisc/Getty Images, © Yuri Arcurs/age fotostock, © Alberto Pomares/iStockphoto, © Bettmann/Corbis, © Dan Eckert/iStockphoto, © Lezlie Sterling/Sacramento Bee/MCT/Newscom, NASA, © digitalsport-photoagency/Shutterstock, © Natphotos/Digital Vision/Getty Images, © Andrey Khrolenok/Shutterstock, © Anne Ackermann/Digital Vision/Getty Images, © Comstock Select/Corbis, © Diego Azubel/Corbis; p. 8 bl: © Ken Karp; p. 31 tr: © Miodrag Gajic/iStockphoto; p. 39 br: © FogStock LLC/Index Open; p. 41 br: © Charles Taylor/Shutterstock; p. 42 tr: © Erich Schlegel/The New York Times/Redux; p. 48 b: © Albert Campbell/Shutterstock; p. 49 cr: © Jose Luis Pelaez Inc./Getty Images; p. 51 tr: © Gary Wales/iStockphoto; p. 52 t: © Ivana Rauski/Fotolia; p. 53 br: © Photos.com Select/Index Open; p. 54 tl: © Andres Rodriguez/Dreamstime.com; p. 57 tl: © Natal'ya Bondarenko/Thinkstock; p. 60 br: © Chen Fu Soh/iStockphoto; p. 61 tr: © Alexander Hafemann/iStockphoto; p. 64 tr: © Maria Nonko/iStockphoto; p. 69 tr: © Buzz Pictures/Alamy; p. 70 tr: © PPL/Shutterstock; p. 72 tr: © Midwest Wilderness/iStockphoto; p. 74 tr: © Henny Boogert; p. 75 tr: © Andrey Khrolenok/Shutterstock; p. 76 tr: © Corbis; p. 78 tr: © Supri Suharjoto/Shutterstock; p. 79 tr: © Ben Blankenburg/iStockphoto; p. 82 tr: © Thomas Northcut/Getty Images; p. 83 tr: © Library of Congress; p. 84 tr: © Kwan Fah Mun/Shutterstock; p. 87 tr: © John Mitchell/Photo Researchers, Inc.; p. 89 tr: © Michelle McNamara/Fotolia; p. 90 tr: © Drazen Vukelic/iStockphoto; p. 98 right: © Australian War Memorial; p. 99 tr: © Ian Waldie/Getty Images; p. 100 tr: © Afaizal/Shutterstock; p. 105 tr: © Christopher Tan Teck Hean/Shutterstock; p. 106 tr: © Christophe Boisvieux/Corbis; p. 107 tr: © Wadia Movietone/Roy Wadia; p. 108 tr: © Brett Atkins/Shutterstock; p. 109 tr: © Lezlie Sterling/Sacramento Bee/MCT/Newscom; p. 110 tr: © Jeremy Woodhouse/Photodisc/Getty Images; p. 113 tr: © Zac Macaulay/Getty Images; p. 115 tr: © Tim McCaig/iStockphoto; p. 116 tr: © Laurentiu Garofeanu/Barcroft USA/Landov; p. 117 tr: © Natphotos/Digital Vision/Getty Images; p. 118 tr: © Michael Habicht/Animals Animals; p. 119 tr: © Tomasz Zachariasz/iStockphoto; p. 120 c: © Don Smetzer/Getty Images; p. 123 tr: © Image Register 112/Alamy; p. 124 tr: © Kate Brooks/Polaris; p. 125 tr: © Ty Allison/Taxi/Getty Images; p. 128 tr: © Diane Diederich/iStockphoto; p. 129 tr: © Pat Wellenbach/AP Images; p. 130 tr: © Jeff Greenberg/Alamy; p. 131 tr:

© Isaac Brekken/AP Images; p. 132 tr: © Dennis MacDonald/Alamy; p. 133 tr: © Mary Stephens/iStockphoto; p. 136 tr: © Steve Hebert/Getty Images; p. 138 tr: © Mary Evans Picture Library/Alamy; p. 139 tr: © Bettmann/Corbis; p. 140 t: © Judith Collins/Alamy; p. 142 tr: © Frank Leung/iStockphoto; p. 143 tr: © Image Source/Jupiter Images; p. 144 tr: © Sue McDonald/iStockphoto; p. 145 tr: © Vincent Yu/AP Images; p. 146 tr: © Yuri Arcurs/age fotostock; p. 148 tr: © Tim Vaughn; p. 149 tr: © Robert & Linda Mitchell; p. 150 tr: © Norbert Wu/Minden Pictures; p. 151 tr: gh5046/Wikipedia; p. 152 tr: © Time Life Pictures/Getty Images; p. 153 tr: © The Tennessean, Mandy Lunn/AP Images; p. 154 tr: © Win McNamee/Getty Images; p. 155 tr: © SW Productions/Brand X/Jupiter Images; p. 156 tr: © Bill Coster/NHPA/Photoshot; p. 159 tr: © Tony Freeman/PhotoEdit; p. 161 tr: © Alberto Pomares/iStockphoto; p. 162 tr: © L. Chang/commons.wikimedia.org; p. 163 tr: © Diego Azubel/Corbis; p. 165 tr: © NASA; p. 166 tr: © Mike Funsch; p. 167 tr: © Christina Dicken/News-Leader; p. 168 tr: © PRENZEL PHOTO/Animals Animals; p. 169 tr: © Lorenz Britt/Jupiter Images; p. 170 tr: © Weather Underground/AP Images; p. 172 tr: © Corrie Davidson, Courtesy Institute of Museum and Library Services; p. 175 tr: © Todd Sowers/LDEO, Columbia University, Palisades, New York; p. 177 tr: © Nailya Shebanova/iStockphoto; p. 178 tr: © www.splashnews.com; p. 179 tr: © Dr. Merlin D. Tuttle/Photo Researchers, Inc.; p. 181 tr: © Aleksey Ignatenko/Shutterstock; p. 183 tr: © Jilly Wendell/Getty Images; p. 184 tr: © Corbis; p. 185 tr: © Reed Hoffmann/AP Images; p. 186 tr: © David Young-Wolff/PhotoEdit Inc.; p. 187 tr: © Anne Ackermann/Digital Vision/Getty Images; p. 188 tr: © Holly Harris/Stone/Getty Images; p. 189 tr: © George Steinmetz/Corbis; p. 190 tr: © Map Resources; p. 191 tr: © Les Stone/Polaris; p. 193 tr: © Joer-Martin Schulze/Action Press/Zuma; p. 194 tr: Harry Baumert © 2006, The Des Moines Register and Tribune Company; p. 195 tr: © Comstock Select/Corbis; p. 196 tr: © Time Life Pictures/Getty Images; p. 197 tr: © ABPL/Animals Animals; p. 198 tr: © Linda Grove/Hulton Archive/Getty Images; p. 199 tr: NASA; p. 200 tr: © Bettmann/Corbis; p. 201 tr: © Bettmann/Corbis; p. 202 tr: © 2006 VStock LLC/Index Open; p. 203 tr: © Dan Eckert/iStockphoto; p. 204 tr: NASA; p. 205 tr: © Howard Grey/Getty Images; p. 206 tr: © Juriah Mosin/Shutterstock; p. 207 tr: © Clara Natoli/Shutterstock; p. 209 tr: © Gary Gershoff/Wireimage/Getty Images; p. 210 tr: © Chang W. Lee/The New York Times/Redux; p. 211 tr: © Steven

Vidler/Corbis; p. 213 tr: © iStockphoto; p. 214 tr: © Michael C. York/AP Images; p. 216 tr: © Bob Elsdale/Getty Images; p. 217 tl: © iStockphoto, tr: © iStockphoto; p. 218 tr: © John Rooney/AP Images; p. 219 tr: © Michel Euler/AP Images; p. 220 tr: © Lebrecht Music & Arts; p. 222 tr: © Courtesy of the Saratoga Springs History Museum; p. 223 tr: © James Steinberg/Photo Researchers, Inc.; p. 224 tr: © Jane Pang/iStockphoto; p. 225 tr: © Reuters/Corbis; p. 226 tr: © Bettmann/Corbis; p. 228 tr: © Bettmann/Corbis; p. 229 tr: © digitalsport-photoagency/Shutterstock; p. 230 tr: © Jim McIsaac/Getty Images; p. 231 tr: © Scholastic Inc.; p. 232 tr: © Bettmann/Corbis; p. 233 tr: © The Granger Collection, New York/The Granger Collection; p. 234 tr: © USGS; p. 235 tr: © NOAA National Severe Storms Laboratory (NSSL) Collection; p. 236 tr: © NASA, ESA, and M.J. Jee (John Hopkins University); p. 237 tr: © Bettmann/Corbis; p. 258 b: © Brennan Linsley/AP Images; p. 259 c: © Juuce/iStockphoto; p. 260 c: © FogStock/Alamy; p. 262 left: © Tamer Yazici/Shutterstock; p. 263 tr: © Museum of London/HIP/The Image Works; p. 264 b: © Thomas Northcut/Getty Images; p. 266 tl: © Stocktrek Images/Getty Images, br: © Laurence Gough/Shutterstock; p. 268 bl: © Willem Dijkstra/Shutterstock; p. 269 t: © Jennifer Ruch/Shutterstock; p. 271 c: © VStock LLC/Index Open; p. 272 left: © Graphi-Ogre/GeoAtlas; p. 273 bl: © Jim McMahon, br: © erikdegraaf fotografie/Shutterstock; p. 275 left: © Brian Evans/Photo Researchers, Inc.; p. 276 right: © Fritz Polking/Dembinsky Photo Associates; p. 277 right: © Jack Fields/Corbis; p. 279 left: © OlgaLIS/Shutterstock; p. 280 left: © North Wind Picture Archives; p. 281 left: © Simon Kwong/Reuters/Corbis; p. 282 right: © Shutterstock; p. 284 left: © Eric Isselée/Shutterstock; p. 285 left: NOAA; p. 286 left: © Oxford Scientific/Getty Images; p. 287 left: © SuperStock,Inc./SuperStock.

Illustrations:

Debbie Palen: pp. 9; 12; 13; 17; 23; 26; 28; 32; 34; 36; 41; 45; 49t; 50; 56; 59; 60t; 64b; 73; 81; 101; 112; 137; 159; 164; 174; 192; 211; 221.

Bill Greenhead: pp. 10; 16; 18; 21; 24; 27; 30; 37; 40; 44; 48t; 52; 55; 58; 62; 66; 68; 80; 94; 95; 122; 134; 135; 141; 160; 176; 180; 227.

Tim Haggerty: pp. 11; 14; 15; 19; 20; 22; 25; 29; 31; 33; 35; 38; 43; 46; 51b; 54; 57b; 63; 65; 67; 92; 93; 96; 102; 114; 147; 173; 182; 208; 215.